The Cut of Men's Clothes
1600–1900

by the same author

THE CUT OF WOMEN'S CLOTHES 1600–1930

French Engraving *c.* 1678.
Jean de Saint-Jean. Coat
worn with petticoat-
breeches and ribbon
accessories.

The Cut of Men's Clothes
1600–1900

by

NORAH WAUGH

ROUTLEDGE
Theatre Arts Books
New York

First published in 1964
by Theatre Arts Books
Printed in Great Britain

Library of Congress Catalog Card Number 64–21658

ISBN 0 87830 025 2

4 6 8 10 9 7 5 3

Contents

Acknowledgments

My grateful acknowledgments are due to: The Victoria and Albert Museum, the London Museum, the Gallery of Costume, Manchester, the Kung. Livrustkammaren, Stockholm, the British Museum, the National Portrait Gallery, the Bibliothèque Nationale, Paris, *The Tailor & Cutter*, *Punch*; and also to: Mr. J. L. Nevinson, Mr. A. A. Whife of *The Tailor & Cutter*, Mrs. Kay West, and to all those who who have helped me prepare this work.

Illustrations

━━━━━━━━━◦◦◦◦◦━━━━━━━━━

PLATES

French engraving *c.* 1678. Jean de Saint-Jean Coat worn with petticoat breeches
and ribbon accessories   *colour frontispiece*

Plates 1a to 7 between pages 48 and 49

1a. 1610–20. Doublet. *Victoria and Albert Museum*

1b. Breeches with canions. *Victoria and Albert Museum*

2a. *c.* 1615. Charles I when Prince of Wales. Doublet and breeches of red satin with
gold and silver pattern and braid trimmings. *National Portrait Gallery*

2b. Henry Rich, 1st Earl of Holland. Doublet and breeches in red cloth. *National
Portrait Gallery*

3. 1620–35. Doublet in green silk damask. *Victoria and Albert Museum*

4. *c.* 1643. Engraving by *Abraham Bosse* to illustrate the plainer style of dress
adopted after Mazarin's edicts against extravagance and foreign imports

5a. *c.* 1645. A caricature of fashion when the doublet and breeches both became short
and boots and boot hose were still worn

5b. *c.* 1654. Doublet, breeches and casaque made for King Charles Gustavus at the
time of his coronation. *Kung. Livrustkammaren, Stockholm*

6a. *c.* 1660. French engraving. Short doublet, petticoat breeches, and cape

6b. *c.* 1675. French engraving. Early type of coat worn over petticoat breeches
Accessories—baldrick and cravat

7. 1680–90. Cravat-ends. *Victoria and Albert Museum*

Plates 8a to 17 between pages 96 and 97

8a. *c.* 1678. French engraving. Great-coat

8b. *c.* 1678. French engraving. A coat retaining the earlier ribbon accessories

8c. *c.* 1685. French engraving. Showing widening of coat skirts and the appearing of
waistcoat sleeves below the shorter coat sleeves

9a. *c.* 1729. Day coats. Bag-wig, worn with a black ribbon round the neck—the
'Solitaire'. *Hérisset, 'Recueil des Différentes Modes du Temps'*

9b. Great-coats. The plaited queue for travelling or military campaigns. *Hérisset,
'Recueil des Différentes Modes du Temps'*

CUTTING DIAGRAMS

TAILORS' PATTERNS

Introduction

The history of costume is buried under such an accumulation of detail that the first principle and main purpose of dress—to clothe the human body—is often lost sight of, and basic shape and cut, which is the real foundation of any costume, is not given its proper importance. Trimmings and accessories are frequently added at the personal whims of individuals or are derived from some trivial happening in high life. These are constantly changing, but the basic silhouette of the dress reflects the whole period during which it is worn, and the changes, which are much slower, come from a continuous evolution of cut which brings it into line with the much larger canvas of the decorative design and the social life and conditions of its period.

Unfortunately, because of their perishable nature, early costumes are so rare and so far apart in date order that it is only since the beginning of the seventeenth century that there have been sufficient specimens in existence to give an authentic sequence of the evolution of cut.

Here in Great Britain we are fortunate in the number of costumes that have been preserved. The Victoria and Albert Museum and the London Museum have large collections, especially interesting for the rarer seventeenth-century suits, and many provincial museums have good specimens from the eighteenth century onwards. Two notable continental collections—the Royal Armoury, Stockholm, and the Royal Collection of Costume, Rosenborg, Denmark—are very valuable because they contain the suits worn by successive kings of Sweden and Denmark, dating from the seventeenth century. As these suits had usually been made for special royal occasions, coronation celebrations, weddings, etc., their rich materials, beautiful gold and silver embroideries and exquisite workmanship, confirm the often almost incredible contemporary descriptions and show how truly magnificent men's clothes used to be.

From the beginning of the seventeenth until the end of the nineteenth century men's clothes can be roughly divided into three main periods: in each the clothes worn reflected the character of their particular period.

(1) 1600–1680. During the first half of the century there were a series of civil wars in France and in 1642 civil war broke out in England. These were bitter days with the

nobility and landlords fighting for their rights and privileges, and the clothes they wore, rigid and stoutly made, suited those troublous times.

(2) 1680–1800. By the end of the seventeenth century there was an established Court in both England and France. The aristocracy had money and leisure to develop their taste, cultivate their lands and adorn their houses and their persons. The clothes of this period dispensed with the earlier stiff protective interlinings and consequently developed an easier and more flowing line. Military uniform was introduced.

(3) 1800–1900. The nineteenth century saw, with the industrial revolution, the rise of the merchant class and the consequent domination of material and purely practical values. Any unnecessary sartorial fluctuations were discarded and men's clothes became stylized and functional.

Part One

1600-1680

1600-1680

At the beginning of the seventeenth century a man's suit of clothes consisted of doublet, breeches, and cape or casaque (cassock).

DOUBLET

The doublet was the main body-garment which men had worn since the Middle Ages and continued to wear until the third decade of the seventeenth century, when it finally disappeared to be replaced by the coat. Throughout its long existence the doublet, originally a military garment, was always very close-fitting and heavily interlined. The body of this doublet was cut with wide shoulder seams and two side seams, set towards the back, and later a centre back seam. At the beginning of the seventeenth century the extra 'peascod' padding in the centre front of the doublet might still be seen, but in the more fashionable doublet this padding was replaced by 'belly-pieces'—that is, two triangular pieces of extra stiffening which formed a lozenge centre front fitting into the slightly pointed waist-line and reaching half-way up the centre front. These belly-pieces are found in all seventeenth-century doublets. The sleeves were straight with epaulettes, and the basque was broken into separate tabs.

About 1620 the waist of the doublet began to rise, and as the body got shorter the tabs became longer and consequently their number was reduced. This type of doublet, fashionable until 1635–40, was usually slashed, or paned, across the chest in the front, across the shoulders in the back, and down the sleeves to the elbow. If there was no slashing the straight centre back seam was left open at the shoulders, and the upper part of the sleeve was wide with the front seam left open to within three or four inches of the wrist.

By the late 1630's the waist was still higher and the tabs were often reduced to four—two front, two back—long enough to be referred to as skirts. Sometimes the centre fronts, as also the centre backs, were cut in one without a waist seam, and one tab was inserted on each side from the high under-arm waist line.

By the 1640's the doublet had been reduced to four pieces only, two fronts and two backs stitched waist length, and a few years later it stopped at the waist. In England and most European countries this short doublet had small tabs round the waist to cover the gap between the doublet and the breeches. In the fashionable French Court it was usually worn very short, exposing a volume of shirt. The typical sleeve of these later doublets was rather wide, usually worn with the front seams open and often only elbow length. The centre back seam was still left open across the shoulders.

BREECHES

Although the Englishman of the sixteenth century was criticized for following foreign fashions and wearing Dutch hose, French hose, Venetian breeches, etc., the last, as well as the square-based trunk hose worn with canions, appear to have been the most popular. Canions were the tight-fitting thigh pieces sewn to the full padded upper hose and were added when knitted stockings came into vogue. The somewhat rigid shape of the trunk hose as worn at the turn of the century was soon replaced by a softer line; they then became very full breeches attached to a wide band just above the knees.

When the waist of the doublet rose the balance of design was kept by reducing the fullness in the breeches, especially round the bottom which now came below the knee, a length more in keeping with the fashionable short boots. The slight fullness below the knee was gathered into a very narrow band.

The straight line of the doublet of the late 1630's was repeated in the long straight breeches. There was still fullness round the waist but none at the bottom, which was often trimmed with loops of braid or ribbon to hide the awkward gap between breeches and boots.

Unfortunately, when in 1645 the doublet shortened the breeches did likewise. This somewhat ridiculous style was, however, soon improved by putting more material into the breeches, which then became so wide that they were called 'petticoat-breeches'. The petticoat-breeches were of two different styles. The legs would be separate and worn over under-drawers, not visible except for their deep flounces, often of lace, which fell over the knee. This was probably a left-over from the wide tops of the boot hose which continued to be worn for a few years even after the boots themselves had been discarded *c.* 1650. These flounces were called 'canons' and were often separate pieces of decoration. The other variation was a skirt, or petticoat, short enough to show the full bloomer-breeches worn underneath, with canons or only with ornamental garters tied in a large bow.

The early method of lacing the breeches to the doublet—by tags round the waist, visible when tied outside—was discarded about 1620. The breeches were then attached by large hooks, sewn on their waistband, which hooked into rings or straps inside the doublet waist.

CAPES, CASAQUES

For full dress a circular cape always accompanied the doublet and breeches, but for travelling or on military campaigns, the cape might be replaced by the casaque. This casaque (or mandilion) was a cape, but cut with two fronts, two backs, and two shoulder pieces. It was cleverly designed so that the fronts and backs could be buttoned together to form a coat, the shoulder pieces becoming sleeves. By the second quarter of the century it had lost its cape-like form and was always worn as a coat, still slit centre back and sides for convenience in riding, and these slits retained their buttons and buttonholes. It had become a very practical garment and could be termed a riding-coat. It is not therefore surprising to find this loose coat being increasingly worn over the extravagant and impractical short doublet and petticoat-breeches.

Except for full dress Court occasions, by the end of the 1660's the coat had come into general use. The next step was to give it more style. Pepys's and Evelyn's 'Persian Coat', Randle Holmes's 'Tunick and Vest' were probably all experiments to that end. The French now called it *Justaucorps*. The doublet lost its stiffness, sometimes it was short, sometimes long, but gradually it took on the role of an undergarment, finally becoming the waistcoat. The petticoat-breeches lost their petticoat, the full bloomer-breeches taking over. Sometimes these had a flounce (canon)—but it was now turned up like a cuff and caught to the legs of the breeches. As the coat gained in importance so the breeches shrank and became simpler. During this transition period, 1660–1680, from doublet to coat, many variations and experiments of style can be seen and it was not until 1680 that the new fashion of coat, waistcoat, and knee breeches was really finally established.

MATERIALS, DECORATION

Fashionable seventeenth-century suits were made from silk materials—satins, damasks, velvets, etc., as well as gold and silver cloths. These as well as the best laces and braids came from Italy. The financial situation in both England and France was such that the cost of importing these materials was prohibitive and many edicts were passed against their use, edicts which, however, the extravagant taste of the period contrived to ignore. The English silk industry was slight, producing chiefly ribbons, while the French silks were of much poorer quality than the Italian. This may explain why these plainer silks were often enriched by embroidery worked in an all-over design, or in wide bands, and the great use of narrow braids and ribbons which could be of local manufacture.

Doublets at the beginning of the century were still cut and pinked. The typical slashed, or paned, doublets, *c.* 1625–40, were often embroidered or assembled from shaped bands whose lines were emphasized by very narrow braids or cords. Although the suit, i.e., doublet, breeches, and cape, was usually of one material and design the doublet itself was sometimes of a richer stuff while the cape and breeches matched.

Throughout the century all the seams of the doublet were covered with a double row of narrow braid. Bows and loops of ribbon first appeared as decoration round the waist when the breeches hooked to the doublet; they took the place of the lacing tags. When the doublet was worn unbuttoned at the waist, loops of ribbon disguised the front opening of the breeches. Soon they were round the bottom of the legs. The fashionable man also scattered bows on his boots, his hat, his gloves and his sword; but it was in the 1650's and 60's on the very full petticoat-breeches that the ribbons really ran riot— loops on the shoulders, round the doublet sleeves, the shirt sleeves, the cravat, round the waist, sides and bottoms of the breeches. Several hundred yards of ribbon might be used to decorate one suit. This extensive use of decoration, which continued during the transition from doublet to coat, was probably a reaction from the sterner days England and France had lived through, which also found expression in the extravagance of the French Court when Louis XIV took control, and the restoration of Court life in England under Charles II, a king who had suffered the indignities of poverty and exile.

CONSTRUCTION OF THE DOUBLET

The outer material of the body of the doublet and the sleeves was always mounted on a very strong linen interlining, which usually had been stiffened with gum or paste (buckram). Sometimes there is an extra strip of this stiffening up the centre fronts, and the collar had usually three layers. The belly-pieces, attached to the interlining, might be of pasteboard or cut from three layers of buckram further stiffened with vertical whalebones. On the right side, where the buttons were, the belly-piece came to the edge of the doublet, while on the left side it was placed about three-quarters of an inch in to allow for buttoning. Small tags with eyelet-holes were stitched a few inches either side of the waist so that the doublet could be tightly laced in to the waist before being buttoned. Inside round the waist, about three inches from the centre fronts, was a narrow band with either eyelet-holes, rings or straps, through which the laces or hooks, sewn to the waistband of the breeches, were fastened. There was usually some padding on the shoulder round the armhole to support the wide shoulder seam.

The early full breeches, as well as being interlined with a woollen material, were mounted on an inner lining, easy at the waist but falling straight down the leg to the requisite length. (No patterns of these inner linings are given in the diagrams as the originals have perished.)

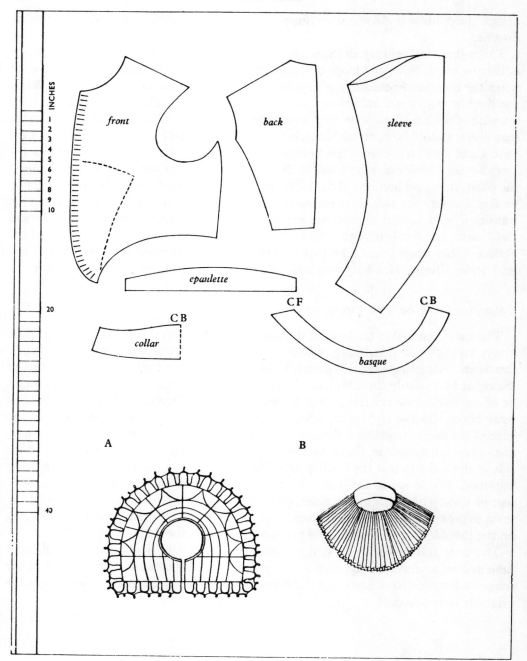

INCHES
1
2
3
4
5
6
7
8
9
10

20

40

front

back

sleeve

epaulette

C F

C B

basque

C B

collar

A

B

DIAGRAM I

Doublet *c.* 1600. *Reconstructed.* The peascod padding of the doublet is graduated from the sides to centre front and is thickest at the waist. All seams, also sleeve seams and round basque, are outlined with two rows of narrow braid.

A. Supportasse, or Underpropper 1605–30. The wire base over which is worn the Ruff or Standing Band (Golilla).

B. Falling Band 1615–40. Several layers of fine lawn, often edged with lace, are gathered on to a deep band.

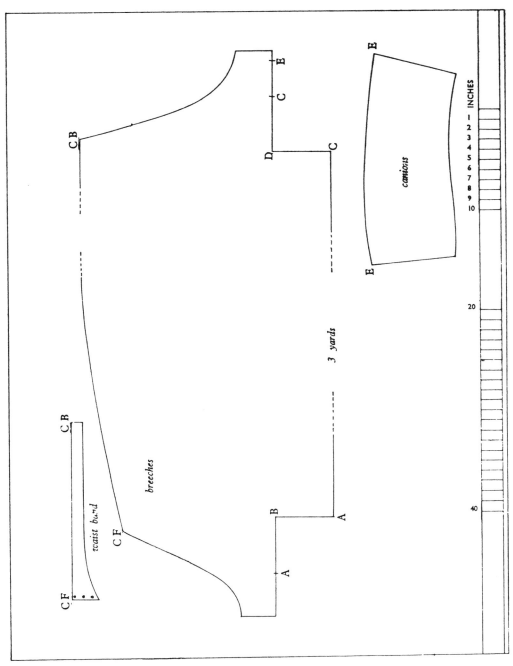

DIAGRAM II

BREECHES 1600–10. *Reconstructed*. The fullness round the waist is set in deep inverted pleats. At the base A B is joined to A B, and C D to C D. The fullness from A to C is sewn to the canions in cartridge pleats.

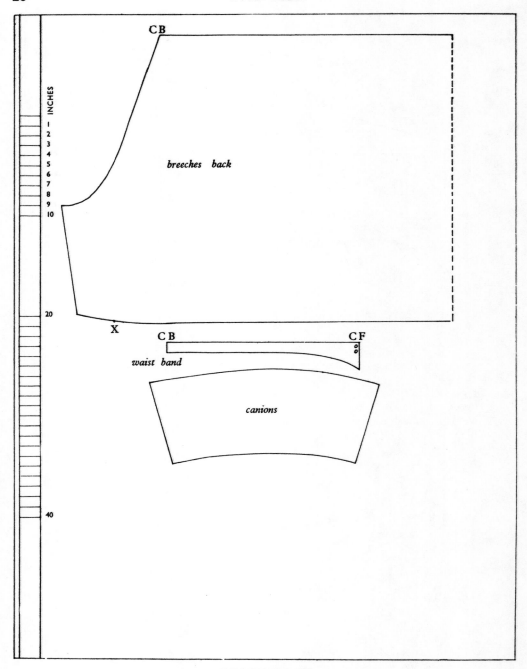

INCHES

1
2
3
4
5
6
7
8
9
10

20

40

CB

breeches   back

X

CB   CF

waist band

canions

DIAGRAM III

DOUBLET AND BREECHES *c.* 1610–20 (see Plate 1). Cream satin over blue silk, both materials cut and pinked. The seams of the doublet, sleeves, edges of epaulettes and tabs, are outlined with two rows of narrow braid. There are 35 buttons up the centre front. The breeches are gathered to the waistband at the top, and to the canions from X to Y. *Victoria and Albert Museum*

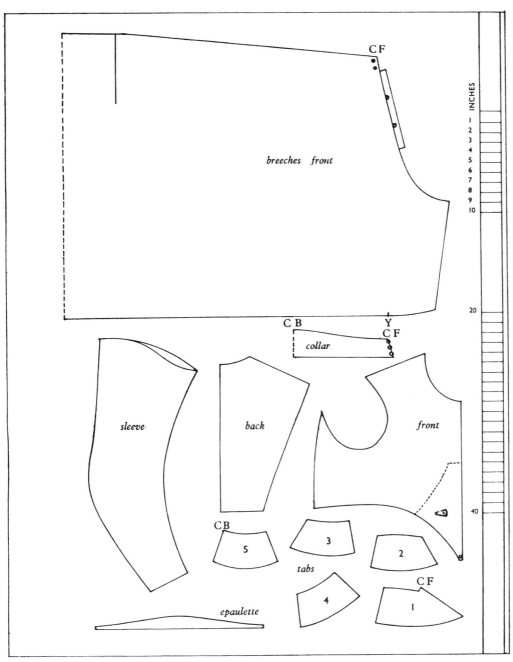

breeches front

CF

CB Y
C F
collar

sleeve

back

front

CB
5

3

tabs

2

4

epaulette

CF
1

INCHES

DIAGRAM III

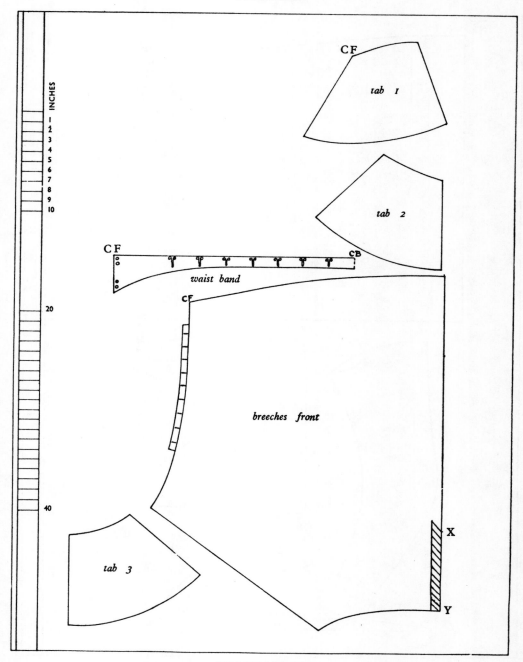

INCHES

1
2
3
4
5
6
7
8
9
10

20

40

CF

tab 1

tab 2

CF   CB
waist band

CF

breeches front

tab 3

X

Y

DIAGRAM IV

DOUBLET AND BREECHES *c.* 1630. Black damask, trimmed with narrow black braid. The fullness round the waist is set in an inverted pleat centre front, and the rest gathered. The bottom of the leg is also gathered onto a narrow band, and the side seams open from X to Y. The hooks fasten into rings sewn inside the waist of the doublet. *Victoria and Albert Museum*

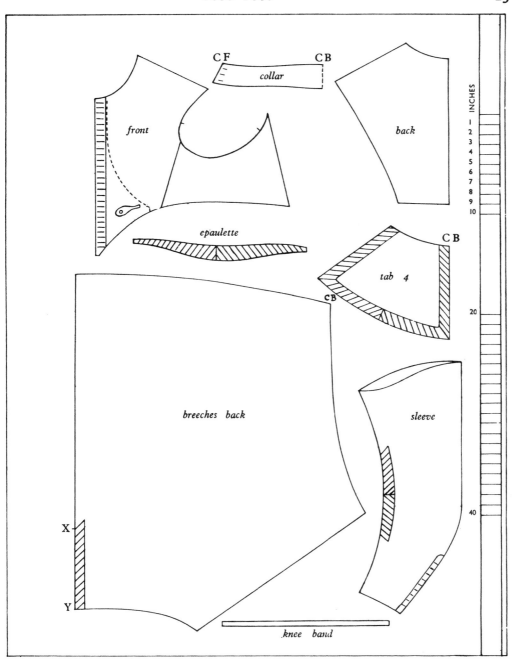

CF   CB
collar

front

back

epaulette

CB
tab 4

CB

breeches back

sleeve

X

Y

knee band

INCHES
1
2
3
4
5
6
7
8
9
10

20

40

DIAGRAM IV

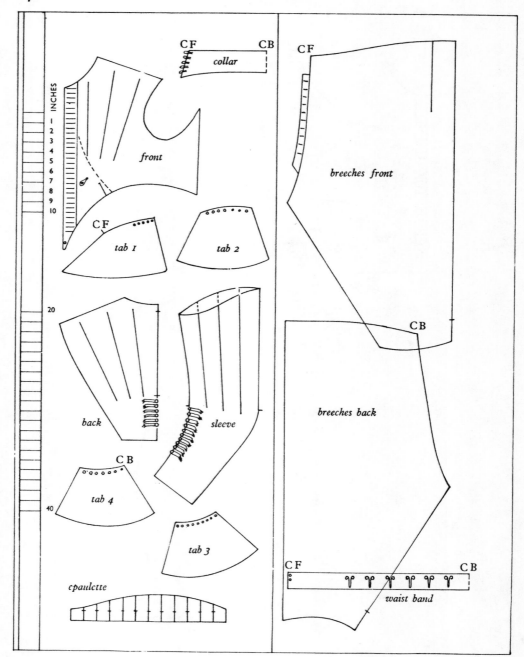

INCHES
1 2 3 4 5 6 7 8 9 10

20

40

CF   CB
collar

front

CF
tab 1

tab 2

back

sleeve

CB
tab 4

tab 3

epaulette

CF

breeches front

CB

breeches back

CF   CB
waist band

DIAGRAM V

DOUBLET 1620–35 (see Plate 3). Green silk damask, trimmed with narrow braid. The eye-let holes in the tabs are for trussing the laces (sewn to the breeches). *Victoria and Albert Museum*

DIAGRAM VI

BREECHES 1630–40. Quilted white satin. (Matching doublet similar to Diagram IV.) The fullness round the waist is set in an inverted pleat centre front and the rest gathered. The side seams are sewn to within $2\frac{1}{2}$ inches from the bottom, which has a slot for a ribbon tie. *Victoria and Albert Museum*

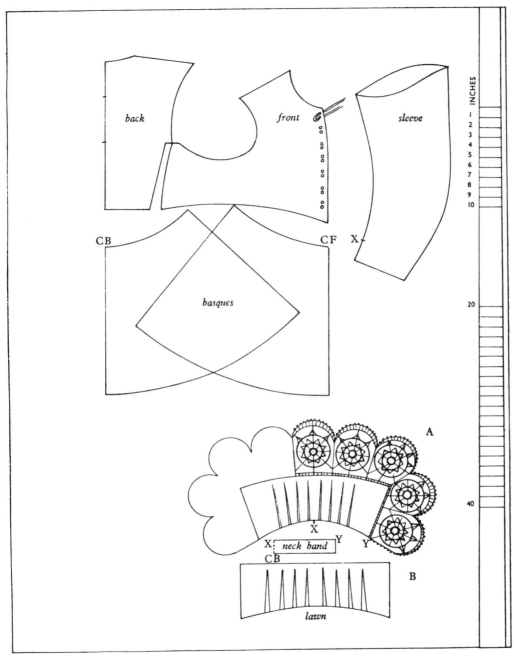

DIAGRAM VII

DOUBLET *c.* 1635. Buff leather. The doublet laces centre front with leather thongs. The sleeves of softer leather with front seams open to X, and bordered with silver lace. *Masner—'Kostümausstellung'*

A. COLLAR, OR BAND 1630–*c.*45. Lawn-edged lace—Italian Reticella, or Flemish.
B. The lawn is darted to fit round the neck.

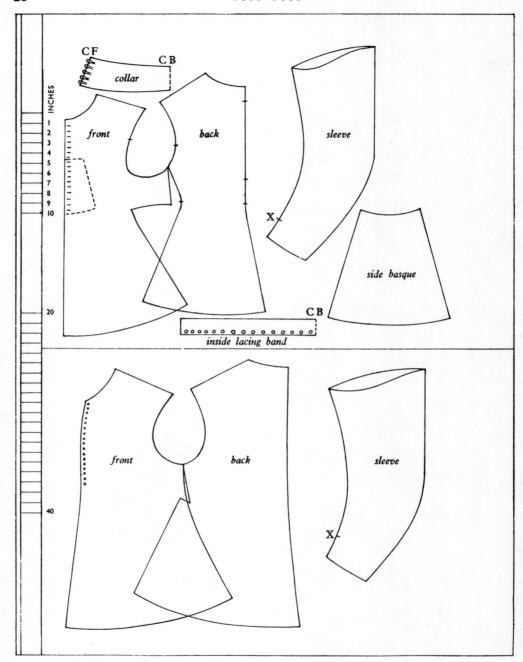

DIAGRAM VIII

DOUBLET *c.* 1635–40. White linen embroidered all over in white linen thread, and edged with narrow bobbin lace. Front and back skirts overlap the side tab one inch. Front seams of sleeves open to X. *Victoria and Albert Museum*

DIAGRAM IX

DOUBLET *c.* 1640. Buff leather. The doublet laces centre front with narrow leather thongs. Front sleeve seams are open to X and bordered with silver lace. *Masner—'Kostümausstellung'*

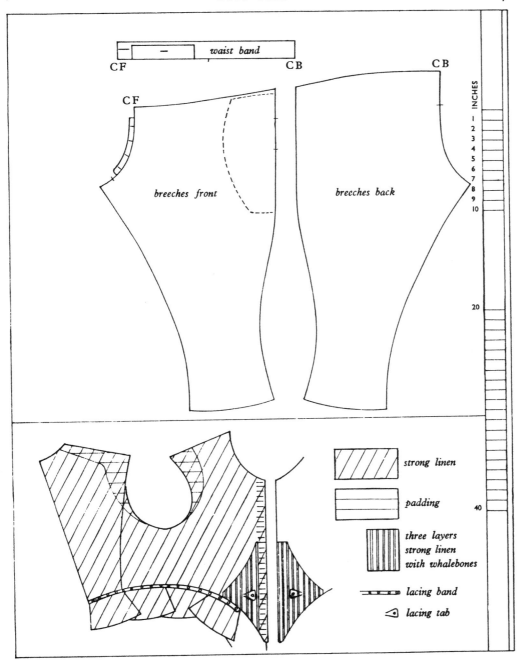

INCHES

1
2
3
4
5
6
7
8
9
10

20

40

strong linen

padding

*three layers
strong linen
with whalebones*

lacing band

lacing tab

DIAGRAM X

BREECHES *c.* 1640. Genoa cut velvet in a coloured floral pattern. The fullness round the waist in an inverted pleat centre front and the rest gathered. Padding is inserted side fronts. *Victoria and Albert Museum*

DIAGRAM XI

CONSTRUCTION OF DOUBLET. The sleeves also are mounted on heavy linen, and the collar has three layers. The belly-pieces are stiffened with paste, or whaleboned.

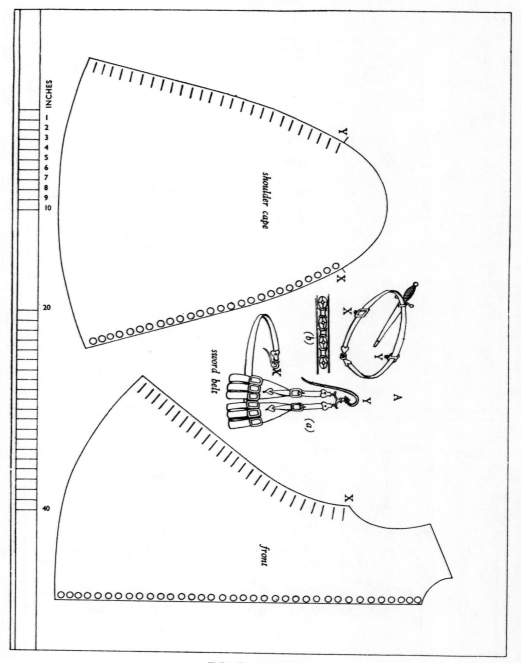

DIAGRAM XII

CASAQUE *c.* 1630. The capes, which are stitched only on the shoulders, can be worn buttoned to make sleeves.

A. SWORD-BELT. Early seventeenth century. Worn round the waist. (*a*) Detail of hanger attached to belt at X and Y. (*b*) Red velvet embroidered in silver over leather.

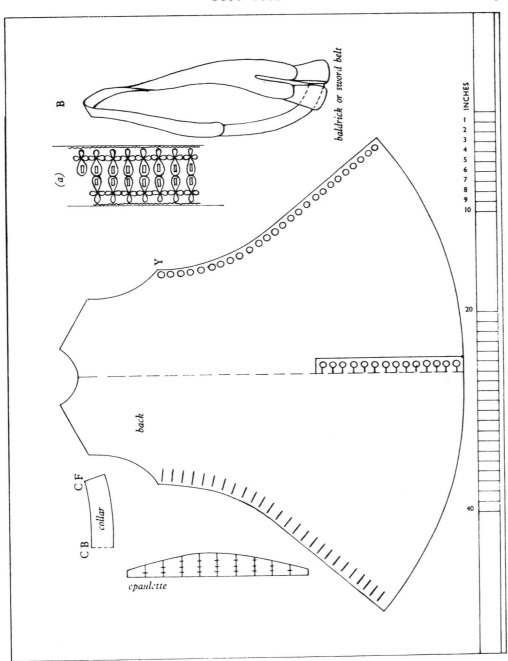

DIAGRAM XII

B. BALDRICK, OR SWORD-BELT 1625–90. Worn over the right shoulder. Later baldricks are longer and wider. (*a*) Detail of pattern worked in brown and silver cord on brown leather.

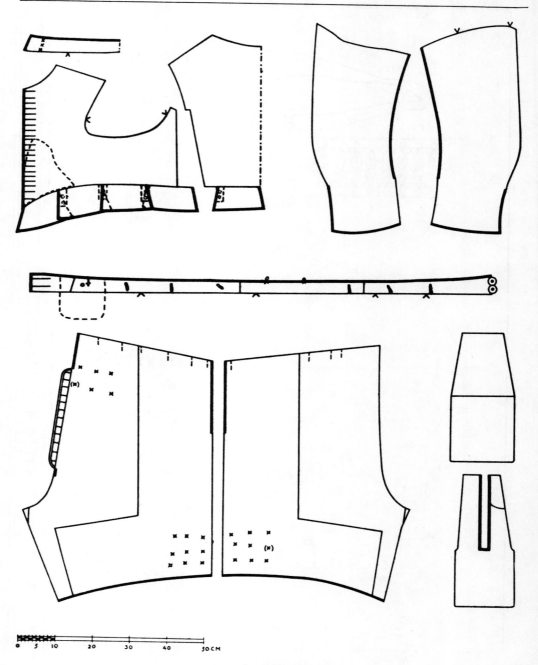

DIAGRAM XIII

DOUBLET, BREECHES, AND CASAQUE 1654 (see plate 5b.) The doublet is of silver brocade, the breeches and casaque of scarlet cloth heavily embroidered in silver. The casaque is lined with silver brocade. The breeches are trimmed with ribbon woven from silver and red silk. *Kung. Livrustkammaren, Stockholm*

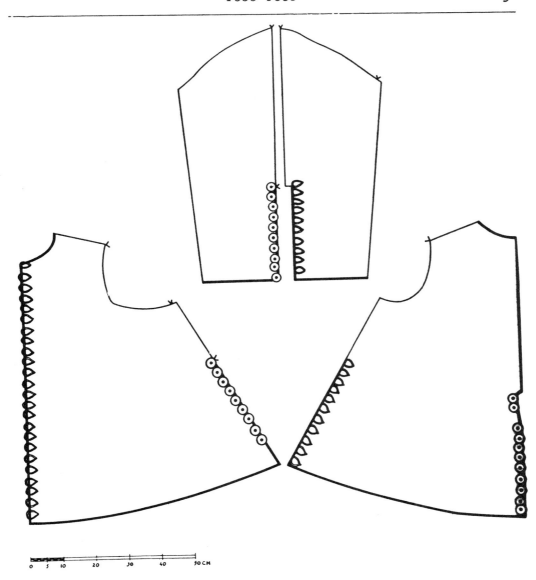

DIAGRAM XIII

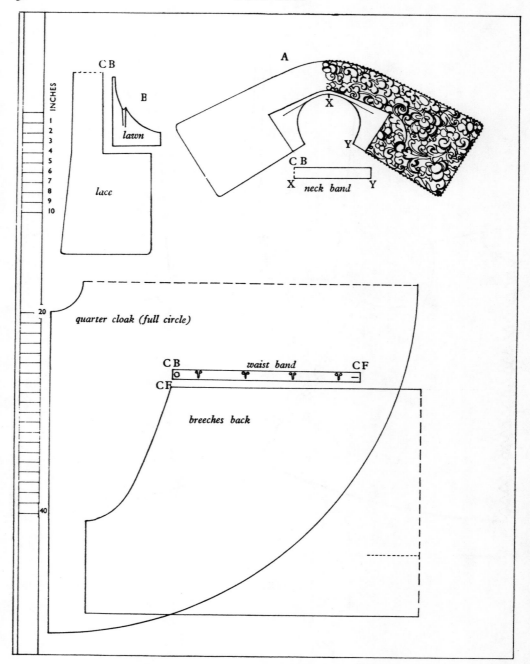

DIAGRAM XIV

DOUBLET, PETTICOAT BREECHES, AND CAPE *c.* **1660.** Cream figured silk tissue. The sleeves of the doublet are made of strips of the silk attached to a wrist band which is trimmed with long loops of coloured silk ribbons—white, yellow, salmon pink and mauve. The breeches have the same ribbon trimming round the waist and on the sides (dotted line). The cape is a full circle. *Verney Collection*

    A. **COLLAR, OR BAND** 1640–70. The back of the collar narrowed as the wigs grew longer. The lace—Venetian Gros Point, or Rose Point.

    B. Lawn inset and lace border.

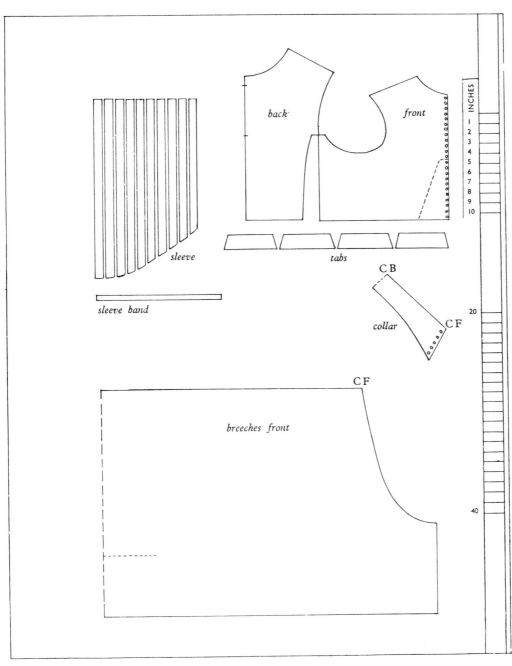

back

front

sleeve

tabs

sleeve band

INCHES
1
2
3
4
5
6
7
8
9
10

20

40

C B

collar

C F

C F

breeches front

DIAGRAM XIV

Seventeenth-century Tailoring

Tailoring is one of the essential crafts whose origin goes back to the dark ages of Western European civilization. From early mediaeval times the importance of this craft was recognized and tailors' guilds were established in all large European towns'. In 1100 Henry I confirmed the royal rights and privileges to the Taylors of Oxford. In London, in 1299, the Guild of Taylors and Linen Armourers was granted arms—linen armour was the tight-fitting padded doublet which was then only worn under chain-mail armour. The Taylors became a Company in 1466, and after 1503, together with other tradesmen, they were incorporated into one of the large city companies—the Merchant Taylors. The tailors of Paris (*Tailleurs de Robes*) received their charter in 1293, but there was also a separate guild for the Linen Armourers (*Maîtres Doubletiers, Pourpointiers*), so in 1358, when the doublet became fashionable civilian wear, a regulation had to be passed to allow the tailors to make civilian doublets (*doublets à vestir*)—*Les Maîtres Tailleurs, Pourpointiers*. From 1346 there was also a guild for tailors who only made hose (*Maîtres Chaussetiers*). In 1588 all these separate guilds were united and became *Les Maîtres Tailleurs d'Habits*, who then had permission to make all the garments worn by both men and women.

Tailoring—the art of designing, cutting, fitting and executing clothes—is a highly skilled craft. It is the most personal and essential of all the applied arts because the artist who creates using cloth, silk and other materials as his medium has always to contend with the human element for the shaping, as well as for the display, of his art. It is an art that is further complicated by the fact that as well as being awkward in shape his model is never static, and the finished product, which should appear pleasing and elegant to a beholder, must also be flexible and comfortable for the wearer to move in.

Cutting out a garment from material is the most important part of the tailor's craft, and from mediaeval times down to the beginning of the nineteenth century the general practice was to cut from patterns. These were flat shapes of the different parts of a garment, made from material (later, usually paper). Simple measurements were also taken and recorded on a long narrow strip of parchment or paper. The tailor laid the pattern on his material and drew it out with chalk, altering the shape where necessary to suit his measurements. This method required years of experience and, for a really good tailor, an inborn gift and a clever eye. It is understandable that good, well-fitting patterns became cherished and highly-valued possessions; in later times it was sometimes stipulated in indentures that the master should give a copy of his patterns to his apprentice, but this was done only on condition of strict secrecy; sometimes they were bequeathed as legacies from father to son. From the beginning of the nineteenth century there were shops in London which sold patterns—a complete set of useful paper models was charged at five pounds; men's frock or lapelled coats with new or old backs, 5s. 6d.; men's breeches or pantaloons, 3s.; etc.

The few early books on tailoring give very simple patterns. Their main purpose was to show how to lay these out in the most advantageous way according to the width of the material used. There are no variations of style and no technical instructions; fitting is never mentioned.

Two of the earliest books on tailoring are Spanish: *Libro de Geometrica Practica y Traca*, Madrid, 1589, Juaan de Alcega; and *Geometrica y Traca*, Madrid, 1618, La Rocha Burguen. In each case the text is meagre; their main concern is the quantity of material required to cut certain garments. A little advice is given to tailors to take careful measurements of their clients: 'The tailor who wishes to cut his clothes well, either for a man or for a woman, should take careful measurements of his clients.' He is also warned of the vagaries of the said clients, who 'very often when a garment is being cut ask it to be made two or three inches shorter and narrower, and when the garments are made, want them longer and fuller, which means that many garments are wasted, and the tailor should allow for this'. Diagrams are given of doublets, breeches, capes, and various ecclesiastical garments—the same simple pattern being repeated in different layouts according to the width of the material (page 39).

The earliest known French work on tailoring is *Le Tailleur Sincère*, Paris, 1671, le Sieur Benist Boullay: 'shewing how to cut all the parts of men's suits, and the quantity of material that each should require—from the age of fifteen years to the greatest height and breadth that a man might have—and also the various types of material. . . . I begin by explaining all the parts that compose a suit. First, that in the doublets there are two fronts, one back and two sleeves, the rest of the suit is the two legs of the breeches, and a cloak; the basques, belt, and collar are not given because they can be cut from the small pieces left over. All the Casaques, Just-au-corps and Soutanes are also of two fronts, one back and two sleeves.'

Text and instructions are slight and not enlightening. The author lays stress on the importance of measurements, but does not say what measurements should be taken: 'Firstly, it is very necessary to observe well a man before measuring him, so as to note his ordinary posture, and that without warning him, for he may stoop naturally or hold himself erect, or else lean on one side or the other; if he expects that you are going to take his measure, he will think he is doing right to hold himself more erect than usual and you will fail with your measure. For, as he is accustomed to stoop, the back part of your garment will be too short, and the front too long. The contrary effects will take place if he stoops more than he usually does, the back will be long and the front short, which is one of the worst faults a coat can have.'

Le Sieur Boullay gives patterns for a variety of garments—royal ceremonial robes, robes for clergy, magistrates and other officials, as well as suits. These include Italian, Spanish and Hungarian types and even a poor man's coat (all these being very similar to the doublets and breeches fashionable in England thirty years earlier). Again, as with the Spanish books, the same simple pattern is repeated in various layouts but with the advance that the patterns also vary in size. The date of publication makes this work interesting as it appeared just when the coat was coming into fashion. His suit patterns consist of:

(1) Doublet (*pourpoint*), petticoat-breeches (*haut-de-chausses*) and cape (*manteau*).
(2) Doublet, petticoat-breeches, and casaque.
(3) Doublet, petticoat-breeches, and coat (*juste-au-corps*).

The last plate of diagrams shows coats to practically all the suits (pages 40, 41, 42).

Encyclopaedias belong to the next century, but the Academy of Armoury, 1688, by Randle Holmes, as well as being 'A Storehouse of Armory and Blazon' contains 'the Instruments used in all Trades and Sciences, together with their Terms of Art'. The section on clothes lists contemporary garments for men, women, children and clergy:

'In a MANS SUITE of cloathes are these several parts: as

THE DOUBLET, it is the whole covering for the upper part of the Man: in which there is these peeces and terms

The two FORE BODIES
The two BACK PARTS

The Waist, is the length from the shoulder to the middle, now in a Doublet it may be the fashion to be

SHORT-WAISTED
SIDE-WAISTED (Long-Waisted)

The SKIRTS, or LAPS, because one lieth a little over another, they are distinguished by the fore skirts, side skirts and hinder skirts; sometimes the custom is to have them more or less, big and little, narrow or short, and large and deep.

The COLLAR is that part as composeth the Neck.

The BELLY-PEECES, the inward stiffning of the Breast of the Doublet.

The Linning, is fine Flaxed or Linnen; called the out lining.

The INNER LINING is Canvice, Buckram, or such like, next to the cloth or stuff; between it and the foresaid Lining.

The WAIST-BAND is a . . . under the skirts to which the straps are fastened.

The EYES, or HOLDERS; are small Wiers made round through which the Breeches hooks are put, to keep them from falling.

STRAPS, are peeces of Leather fastned to the waistband instead of Eyes, or holders.

WAISTCOAT, is a close Garment worn under a Doublet and within the Waistband of the Breeches.

The SLEEVES, are the covers of the Arms and are of diverse fashions. . . .

SLEEVE BANDS, the lowest part of the sleeves next the wrist.

TURN UPS, or CUFFS: are the turning up of the end of the Doublet next the hand. . . .

BUTTON-HOLES, are such long slitt holes whipped about with a Loop at each end, as are in the left part of the Fore-body, and at the sleeve bands, to receive the Buttons on the right side, and to keep it close together.

The FACEING, is to Face the sleeve bands, is to adorn the turns up with some other sort of Stuff or Silk, than the Suit of Cloathes is made off;

The BREECHES, is that part of cloathing, which covers a Man from his Waist to his Knees; of the fashion of them there is many extent, I shall tell of some few:

The SPANISH BREECHES, are those that are stret and close to the Thigh, and are buttoned up the sides from the knee with about ten or twelve buttons; anciently called TROWSES.

The SAILERS BREECHES, are full and gathered both in the waist and at the Knees, standing full out.

The OPEN BREECHES, are such as are full and wide and not gathered at the knees, but hang loose and open.

The PANTILOON BREECHES

The TRUNK BREECHES

The PETICOAT BREECHES, are short and wide Coats with waist bands, having no petition, or sowing up between the Legs: but all open like a short Peticoat, from whence they are named.

TRIMING, is any thing put on, or about the Doublet, or Breeches: whereby they are adorned and made more Gent, whether it be Ruffles, Laces, Ribbons, Buttons, Loopes, Scalloping, etc.

In the BREECHES, there are several parts:

The WAISTBAND

The HOOKS

The COTTONINGS, is that with which the cloth or outward stuff of the Breeches are Lined.

The DRAWERS, are Linnen Breeches worn under the Breeches which are tied about the waist and either above or under the Knees.

The POCKETS, are little bags let in the sides of the Breeches to put or carry any small thing in. . . .

LOOSE GARMENTS usually worn over the Doublet and Breeches are such as these following:

A STREET-BODIED COAT, this is close to the Body and Arms, and is usually worn without a Doublet, having under it a Waistcote with side or deep skirts almost to the Knees. These Kind of Waist coats are called CHATES: because they are to be seen rich and gaudy before, when all the back is no such thing.

A VEST, is a kind of wide Garment reaching to the knees open before and turned up with a Facing, or lining, the Sleeves wrought to the Elbows and there turned up with a round facing; under it was worn another side skirted Coat made fit to the Body after the manner of a Doublet, which was called a Tunick: the sleeves of it were narrow and rought below the middle of the Arm, where it was all beset with knots of Ribbons: about the middle was worn a Silken Girdle, which was called a Soan, or Sash:

The Vest was the form of the Russian Embassedors loose Coat when he first came to England, shortly after King Charles the Seconds return from Exile, which Garb was so taken too, that it became a great fashion and wear, both in Court, City and Country.

A JACKET, or JUMPE, or loose COAT: it extendeth to the Thighs is open or buttoned down before, open or slit up behind half way: the Sleeves reach to the Wrist having the turn up sometimes round, then with Hounds Ears, and another time square.

A COAT, or RIDING COAT: is a full Coat both wide and side (long) with long and wide Sleeves to be drawn over other kinds of Garments.

A CLOAK is round in compass, and having a Cape distinguished from another sort of covering without a cape, called a Rochet, or Mantle.

A MANTLE, is a round thing made of any stuff, having a round hole in the middle, and so is cut through to the hole, which being put about the neck hangs round about the wearer, which according to the fashion, is large, or little, faced or laced, etc.

Several parts of a BAND:

The HOLLOWING of the band, the rounding it for the neck.

The STOCK that goes round about the Neck.

The CLOCKS, the laying in of the cloth to make it round, the Plaits.

The STRINGS and BUTTONS.

RUFFS are generally cloth folded by Art into sets, or turning, for two or three heights or doublings of cloth.

A CRAVATT is another kind of adornment for the neck being nothing else but a long Towel put about the Collar, and so tyed before with a Bow knot, this is the Original of all such Wearing; but now by the Art and Invention of the Seamsters, there is so many new ways of making them, that it would be a Task to name them, much more to describe them.

PATTERNS, Paper cut in fashions according as the work is to be made.'

Randle Holmes gives several variations of sleeves and adds after one of them: 'as it is now in fashion by the Gallants of our Age, for this present year 1680, but how long it will continue, the Taylor is the only knowing Man to judge of it; for indeed we are all his Apes, delighting in that Dress he puts us in, be it never so ridiculous, to put us out of our comely shapes.'

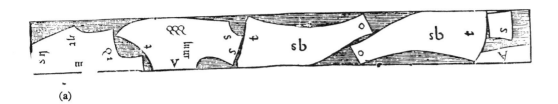

(a)

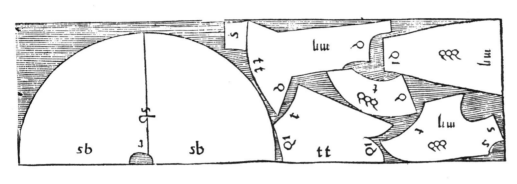

(b)

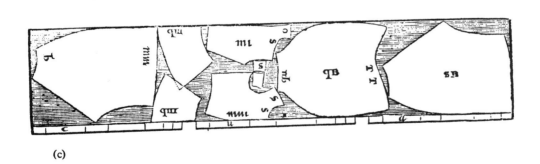

(c)

1. *Libro de Geometrica Practica y Traca*, Juaan de Alcega, Madrid, 1589.
    (a) Doublet with open sleeves.
    (b) Doublet and cape with hood.

    Geometrica y Traca, La Rocha Burguen, Madrid, 1618.
    (c) Doublet and breeches.

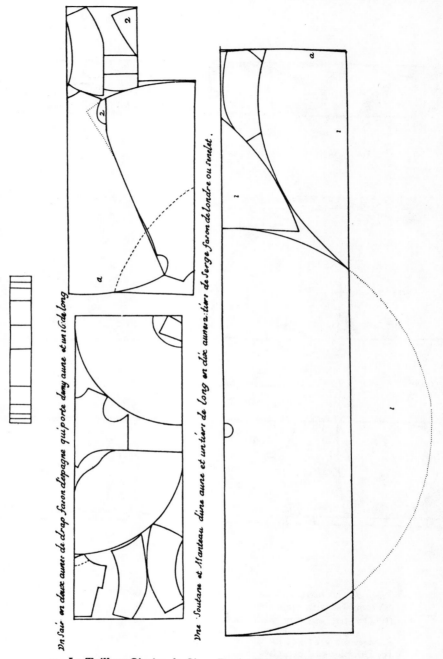

2. *Le Tailleur Sincère,* le Sieur Benist Boullay, Paris, 1671.
     A doublet in Spanish cloth.
     A soutane and cape in London serge.

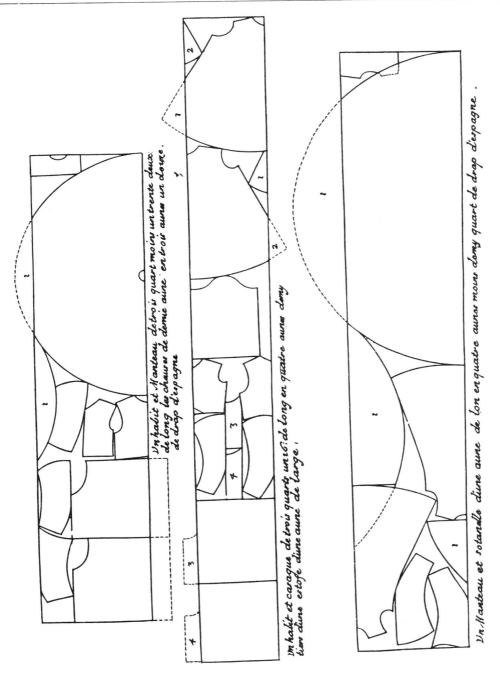

3. *Le Tailleur Sincère*

A suit—doublet, breeches, and cape in Spanish cloth.
A suit—doublet, breeches and casaque.
A cloak and sotanelle in Spanish cloth.

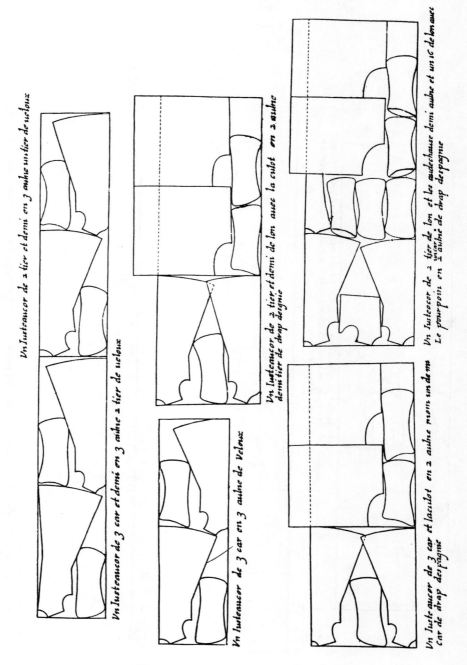

4. *Le Tailleur Sincère*
Three coats in velvet.
Two coats with breeches in Spanish cloth.
A coat, doublet and breeches in Spanish cloth.

Quotations from Contemporary Sources

France—The French, if we respect the time of these late Civill wars, weare light stuffes and woollen cloth, with a doublet close to the body, and large easie breeches, and all things rather commodious for use, than brave of ornament; and scoffed at those who came richly attired to the Campe, or wore long haire. But if wee consider their apparrell before the misery of the said civill warres, we shall find them authors to us English, of wearing long haire, doublets with long bellies to the navell, ruffes hanging downe to the shoulders, and breeches puffed as big as a tunne, with all like wanton levities. In time of peace, Gentlemen weare mixed and light colours, and silk garments, laid with silke lace, and sattens, commonly raced, and stockings of silke, or of some light stuffe, but never woollen or worsted (which only Merchants weare), and imbrodered garments, with great inconstancy in the fashion. . . . And howsoever the Law forbids to weare silke lace upon silke stuffes, yet the execution of the Law being neglected, they ever offend more or lesse, according to the libertie of the time, against the old Law, never yet abolished, but rather in time worne out of respect. . . .

England—The English I say are more sumptuous than the Persians because despising the golden meane, they affect all extremities. For either they will be attired in plaine cloth and light stuffes, (alwayes provided that every day without difference their hats of Bever, their shirts and bands of the finest linnen, their daggers and swords guilded, their garters and shooe roses of silke, with gold and silver lace, their stockings of silke wrought in the seams with silke or gold and their cloakes in Summer of silke, in Winter at least all lined with velvet), or else they daily weare sumptuous doublets and breeches of silke or velvet, or cloth of gold or silver, so laid over with lace of gold or silke, as the stuffes (though of themselves rich) can hardly be seene. The English and French have one peculiar fashion, which I never observed in any other part, namely to weare scabbards and sheaths of velvet upon their rapiers and daggers. . . . If I should begin to set downe the variety of fashions and forraign stuffes brought into England in these times, I might seeme to number the starres of Heaven and sands of the sea.

FYNES MORYSON *An Itinerary*

1617

He'el have an attractive Lace,
And Whalebone-bodyes, for the better grace.
And nit spare dyet, on no sustance feed,
But Oatmeall, Milke, and crums of Barley-bread.
Use Exercise untill at last he fit
(With much adoe) his Body into it.

HENRY FITZ-JEOFFREY, *Notes from Black-Fryers*

1631

Charles Moreau, tailor to Louis XIII

Suit comprising—Doublet of silver cloth embroidered with small flowers Milanese style, with slashes set close together; lined with brown Venetian tabby and bordered with gold and silver lace and a braid laid beside it; 60 buttons of gold and silver thread and buttonholes of the same thread; braid on the sleeve; a piece of coarse canvas, a piece of canvas. Breeches in brown Venetian tabby decorated with braid and 84 buttons down the side seams. Cloak of brown Venetian tabby, lined with cloth of silver embroidered with small gold flowers, and decorated with 25 rows of braid like the rest of the suit. (8½ aunes cloth of silver, 12¾ aunes Venetian tabby, 70 aunes lace, 260 aunes braid —70 for the doublet and 190 for the breeches and cloak.)

(1 aune—1·188 metre)

HIPPOLYTE ROY, *La Vie, la Mode et le Costume au XVII Siècle*

1630's

Louis XIII was skilled in many trades. He was a good barber; one day he shaved off all his officers' beards, only leaving a little tuft of hair on their chins. After that all who were not too old did the same and kept only their moustaches.

Florence—A young man had a doublet made and did not think to have the slashes stitched. One day the Grand Duchess and Mademoiselle de Guise happened to pass by and when they saw this man standing in a doorway they burst out laughing at his ridiculous appearance—his body and arms were so covered with threads that he looked as if he were dressed in a spider's web.

TALLEMANT DES REAUX, *Historiettes*

1638   BILL FROM THE VERNEY PAPERS

	16 Mar. 1638
For Collr & belypeeces & hookes & eyes to a buffe coate . .	00 : 02 : 06
For lyneings to yr hose	00 : 05 : 00
For makeing ye buff coate with 2 paire of sleeues & hose last all ouer	01 : 15 : 00

More for 2 shambo skins to make a par sleeues	00 : 12 : 00
For buckrum to ym	00 : 02 : 00
For gould & silluer Butts to yr 2 paire of sleeue hands & ye hoase befor	00 : 03 : 00

1638

I have much wondered why our English above other nations should so much doat upon new fashions, but more I wonder at our want of wit that we cannot invent them ourselves; but when one is growne stale run presently over into France to seeke a new. . . . Hence came your slashed doublets (as if the wearer were cut out to be carbonado'd upon the coales) and your half-shirts, pickadillies (now out of request), your long breeches narrow towards the knees like a pair of smith's bellows, the spangled garters pendent to the shooe, your perfumed perrukes, or periwigs, to show us that lost hair may be had again for money; with a thousand such fooleries unknown to our manly forefathers.

HENRY PEACHAM, Truth of our Times

1644

No one is more changeable than the French: sometimes their hats mount high, sometimes sink low, sometimes their basques are large, sometimes small, their breeches long or short: as to collars, our fathers wore small simple ones, while we began with circles of cardboard over which we laid a starched collar, after that we had a kind of unstarched cape which reached almost to the elbow, and then after that collars became smaller and of a reasonable size, though at the same time there were large tubular-pleated ruffs with enough linen in them to make the sails of a windmill: now these are all discarded and our collars are so small that they are like sleeve cuffs.

Wide bucket-tops are now only seen on heavy boots, the lighter boots worn to-day have dropped down to the spurs, and have only a peak in front and behind. As to the canons displayed above the boots—we like them very large and of fine starched lawn although they then resemble paper lanterns. And we like them even more ornate, of two or three layers of fine lawn or linen, and better still if they are trimmed with two or three rows of *point de Gènes*, which should be the same as for the *jabot*. You know that ribbons and points are called *la petite oye*, and the opening of the shirt in front is called the *jabot*, and it must always be trimmed with lace, for it is only an old fogey who buttons his doublet all the way down. Let's go back to the boots: they must always be long in the foot even if that is extravagant and against nature. When high boots came into fashion, hats were worn with such high pointed crowns that a coin could cover the top, but that has suddenly changed and now they are low and round, but the long boots remain which shows how popular they are. Then the spurs—they must be of heavy silver, and you must keep changing their design without heeding the cost. Those who wear silk stockings should always have English ones, and the garters and shoe rosettes should be as fashion dictates.

There are certain small etceteras which cost little but show elegance (*galanterie*), as for example: placing in the hat a beautiful ribbon, gold or silver, sometimes mixed with coloured silk; and in front of the breeches seven or eight beautiful satin ribbons of the most brilliant colours possible. You might say that this display of trimmings turns your person into a shop exhibiting its wares, however, this is what is worn and this fashion of ribbon trimmings adds very much to the elegance of a man, and that is why they are called *galants*.

Les Loix de la Galanterie

1649

Oxford—The new commers also (who mostly were very meane and poore at their first coming) having gotten into good fellowships, became wondrous malepert and saucy, especially to the old stock remayning. They went in half shirts, appearing at their brest and out at sleeves, great bands with tassell band-strings, and Spanish leather boots with lawne or holland tops.

1663

A strange effeminate age when men strive to imitate women in their apparell, viz. long periwigs, patches in their faces, painting, short wide breeches like petticoats, muffs, and their clothes highly sented, bedecked with ribbons of all colours.

The Life and Times of ANTHONY WOOD

1662

Once and for all I should explain what is a *juste-au-corps à brevet*. When the king (Louis XIV) was first in love with Mme. de la Vallière and no longer kept it secret, the Court was at Saint-Germain, and Versailles was still the small hunting-lodge built for Louis XIII. The king with a few friends used to go there once or twice a week to spend part of the day with Mme. de la Vallière, so he designed a blue coat, lined with red, and with a red waistcoat, both embroidered with a special design; he gave a dozen of them to those friends he allowed to accompany him on these little private visits to Versailles; only those who had such coats could go with him without first asking permission. Afterwards the number of these coats was extended to forty, but never exceeded that number; when one became vacant, the king granted the favour of wearing it by a brevet issued by the State Secretary of the King's Household, and from that it was called a *juste-au-corps à brevet*. They gave no special privileges or entrées; their only distinction was that they could be worn during times of mourning and were allowed when gold and silver trimming on coats was prohibited.

DANGEAU, *Journal* (Note by SAINT-SIMON)

1660–6

1660. May 24. Up, and made myself as fine as I could, with the linning stockings on and wide canons that I bought the other day at Hague.

1661. April 6. Among other things met with Mr. Townsend, who told of his mistake the other day, to put both his legs through one of his knees of his breeches, and went so all day.

1662. June 12. I tried on my riding-cloth suit with close knees, the first that ever I had; and I think they will be very convenient, if not too hot to wear any other open knees after them.

1663. May 9. At Mr. Jervas's, my old barber, I did try two or three borders and perri-wiggs, meaning to wear one; and yet I have no stomach (for it), but that the pains of keeping my hair clean is so great.

May 10. (Lord's day). Put on a black cloth suit with white lynings under all, as the fashion is to wear, to appear under the breeches.

Oct. 30. At my periwigg-maker's, and there showed my wife the periwigg made for me.

Nov. 2. I heard the Duke say that he was going to wear a perriwigg; and they say the King also will. I never till this day observed that the King is mighty gray.

Nov. 3. Home, and by and by comes Chapman, the periwigg-maker, and upon my liking it, without more ado I went up, and there he cut off my haire, which went a little to my heart at present to part with it; but, it being over, and my perriwig on, I paid him £3 for it; and away went he, with my own haire, to make up another of it.

Nov. 8. (Lord's day). To church, where I found that my coming in a perriwigg did not prove so strange as I was afraid it would, for I thought that all the church would presently have cast their eyes all upon me, but I found no such thing.

1666. Oct. 8. The King hath yesterday in Council declared his resolution of setting a fashion for clothes, which he will never alter. It will be a vest, I know not well how; but it is to teach the nobility thrift, and will do good.

Oct. 13. To White Hall, and there the Duke of York was just come in from hunting. So I stood and saw him dress himself, and try on his vest, which is the King's new fashion, and he will be in it for good and all on Monday next, and the whole Court: it is a fashion, the King says, he will never change.

Oct. 15. This day the King begins to put on his vest, and I did see several persons of the house of Lords and Commons too, great courtiers, who are in it; being a long cassocke close to the body, of black cloth, and pinked with white silk under it, and a coat over it, and the legs ruffled with black riband like a pigeon's leg: and, upon the whole, I wish the King may keep it, for it is a very fine and handsome garment.

Oct. 17. The Court is all full of vests, only my Lord St. Albans not pinked, but plain black; and they say the King says the pinking upon whites makes them look too much like magpies, and, therefore, hath bespoke one of plain velvet.

Nov. 4. (Lord's day). My taylor's man brings my vest home, and coat to wear with it, and belt and silver-hilted sword; so I rose and dressed myself, and I like myself mightily in it, and so do my wife . . . and so, it being very cold, to White Hall, and was mighty fearfull of an ague, my vest being new and thin, and the coat cut not to meet before, upon my vest.

SAMUEL PEPYS, *Diary*

1664

I would choose the loose Riding Coat, which is now the *Mode,* and the Hose which his Majesty often wears; or some fashion not so pinching as to need a Shooing-horn with the Dons, nor so exorbitant as the Pantaloons, which are a kind of Hermaphrodite and of neither Sex: and if at any time I fancy'd them wider, or more open at the knees for the Summer, it should be with a mediocrity, and not to set in plaits as if I were supported with a pair of Ionic pillars, or the gatherings of my Grandames loose Gown.

JOHN EVELYN, *Tyranus, or The Mode*

1666

Oct. 18. To Court. It being the first time his Majesty put himself solemnly into the Eastern fashion of vest, changeing doublet, stiff collar, bands and cloake, into a comely vest, after the Persian mode, with girdle or straps, and shoe strings and garters into bouckles, of which some were set with precious stones, resolving never to alter it, and to leave the French mode, which had hitherto obtain'd to our greate expence and reproch. Upon which divers courtiers and gentlemen gave his Majesty gold by way of wager that he would not persist in this resolution. I had sometime before presented an invective against that unconstancy, and our so much affecting the French fashion, to his Majesty, in which I tooke occasion to describe the comliness and usefulnesse of the Persian clothing, in the very same manner his Majesty now clad himselfe. This pamphlet I intitl'd 'Tyrannus, or the Mode', and gave it to his Majesty to reade. I do not impute to this discourse the change which soon happen'd, but it was an identity that I could not but take notice of.

JOHN EVELYN, *Diary*

1664

BILL FROM THE WOBURN PAPERS

James Blaiklaw

To the Right Honnoble William Russell, Esq   Febrii 2

For Canvas & Stiffining to A Pantalon drogget Hose & doublet .	0 : 4 : 6 :
For Gallanne Looplace Ribbin to ye Knees & Collr . . .	0 : 8 : 6 :
For Pokkets & Bellepeeces	0 : 2 : 8 :
for silk	0 : 3 : 0

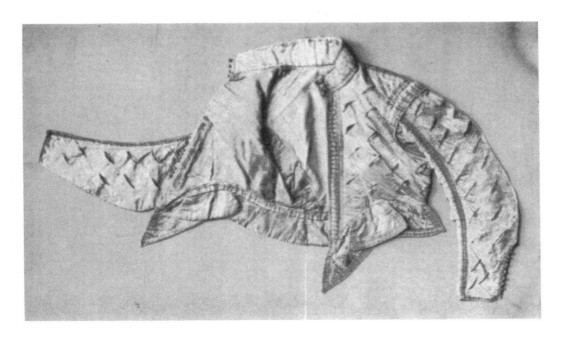

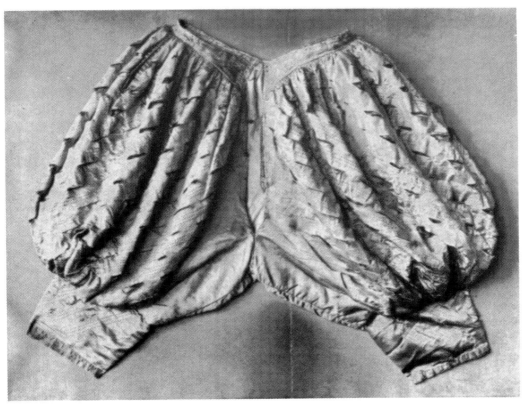

PLATE I

1610–20. (*above*) The belly-piece and band with lacing eyelets can be seen on the inside of this doublet. (*below*) Breeches with canions. This suit is patterned by slashes and pinking. (See Diagram III)

Victoria and Albert Museum

PLATE 2

(*left*) *c.* 1615. Charles I when Prince of Wales; attributed to Abraham Blijenberch. Doublet
and breeches of red satin with gold and silver pattern and braid trimmings
(*right*) *c.* 1635. Henry Rich, 1st Earl of Holland; studio of Daniel Mytens. Doublet and
breeches in red cloth which is barely visible under the rows of gold and silver braid

National Portrait Gallery

PLATE 3
The eyelet holes round the waist are for trussing laces. (See Diagram V)
Victoria and Albert Museum

PLATE 4

c. 1643. Engraving by *Abraham Bosse* to illustrate the plainer style of dress adopted after Mazarin's edicts against extravagance and foreign imports. The hair at this time was worn with a longer lock, or little plait, on the left side—the 'Cadenette'

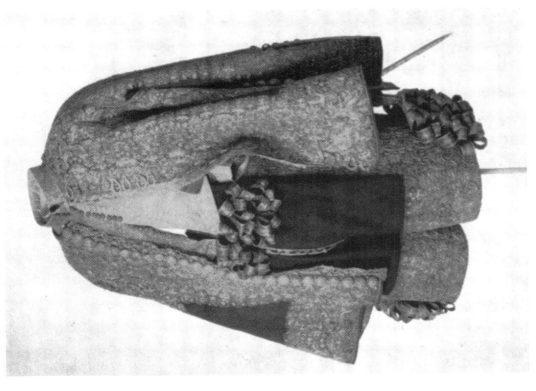

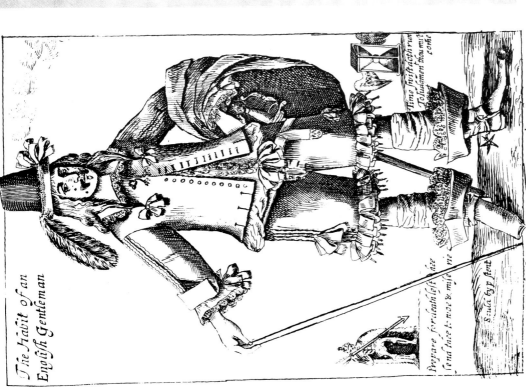

The Habit of an English Gentleman

Prepare for death &
send sure it not & mile sue

Sould byp Hent

Time trusts acth runs
To lula men thou my
come

PLATE 5

(*left*) *c.* 1645. A caricature of fashion when the doublet and breeches both became short and boots and boot hose were still worn. (*right*) 1654. (See Diagram XIII.) This doublet, breeches, and casaque were one of the suits made for King Charles Gustavus at the time of his coronation

Kung. Livrustkammaren, Stockholm

PLATE 6

(*left*) *c.* 1660. French Engraving. Short doublet, petticoat breeches, and cape. The fashion of longer hair meant that wigs were increasingly worn. (*right*) *c.* 1675. French Engraving. Early type of coat worn over petticoat breeches. Accessories—baldrick and cravat

PLATE 7

1680–90. Cravat-ends. Neckcloths became fashionable when the collarless coat came into fashion *c.* 1665, and were called 'cravats'. The name is said to be derived from Croat as such neckcloths were first seen on Louis XIV's regiment of Croat mercenaries. A strip of fine lawn was wrapped round the neck and knotted or tied in front with a narrow ribbon. The fashionable decorated the ends with deep lace, and the tie became a rosette of ribbons. The lace-trimmed ends and rosette were often separate from the cravat. The battle of Steinkirk, 1692, when the French troops were caught unprepared, brought in the fashion of leaving the long ends untied, one of which was passed through the sixth buttonhole of the coat. In the 1720's the cravat was shortened and fastened tightly round the neck, but the long loose type continued to be worn by older men and the poorer classes. The sporting type of cloth coats of the end of the eighteenth century were always accompanied by the cravat, or a folded kerchief, wound loosely round the neck, then knotted or tied in a bow

Victoria and Albert Museum

for Callico	0 : 5 : 0 :
For Sisseing	0 : 3 : 0 :
For Buttons	0 : 5 : 0 :
for Tagging 50 doz of points & Ribbins	0 : 12 : 6 :
for Makeing the Sute to yor Honnor	0 : 12 : 0 :
for Broune Cambrick to Make a pr of Pantalon topps & Stokkings .	1 : 12 : 0 :
for Ribbin with silk & Makeing ye Topps & Stokkings . . .	0 : 6 : 8 :
For Makeing up ye triming wth ye Hatb. Gartr. & 2 pr double stiffind shoeknotts	0 : 5 : 0
For Buckrō Gallanne & Sisseing to A Scarlet Camlet Justacor Linde with Tabee	0 : 5 : 0 :
For 12 dozn of silvr Buttons	1 : 10 : 0 :
for silvr Chaen to ye Button Holls & Looplaces . . .	0 : 12 : 6 :
for scarlet Silk Ingrainde	0 : 4 : 0 :
For Makeing the Justacor to yor Honnor	0 : 10 : 0

1680

BILL FROM THE VERNEY PAPERS

For A shouldr knott sword knott and Sleeue knotts of Rich Scarlett gold and Sillue 16d and 16 Scarlett Satten Ribbon . . .	09 : 00 : 00
For 12 knotts of narrow Ribbon to ye Camions of the Breeches .	01 : 18 : 00
For A payre of orangery Gloves	01 : 01 : 06
For A Scarlett gold and Silluer fringe to trimme them . .	05 : 00 : 00
For Faceing to them and fringing them	00 : 05 : 06
For A payre of Silke Stockings	00 : 14 : 00
For A pearle Couller tabby belt with Silluer Locks . . .	00 : 16 : 00
	18 : 15 : 00

Part Two

1680-1800

1680-1800

COAT

On its first appearance for general wear, *c.* 1660, the coat was rather a dull garment as far as cut was concerned. It had two fronts and two backs, with straight side seams which were stitched to just below the waist—this fashion of leaving the skirts open was continued in all coats until almost the end of the eighteenth century. It accommodated the sword, which hung from a belt worn under the coat, the hilt coming through the side vent and the point through the centre back. The sleeves were wide—elbow length with a turn-back which formed a cuff. It had no collar. During the 1670's and 80's the coat acquired a straighter and more elegant line by being more shaped on the under-arm and centre back seams. The sleeves also became more fitting and reached just below the elbow with long narrow cuffs—'hounds' ears' cuffs. The early habit of adding a variety of trimmings and accessories lingered on and they were an essential part of the design of these early simply-cut coats.

During the 1690's the coat gained in volume. The side skirts were swung out, the sleeves became fuller and the cuffs much wider and deeper and now cut separate. The emphasis was moving from ornamentation to the changing subtleties of cut which was to give such distinction and style to all the coats of the coming century.

It was probably about 1700 that the extra width at the sides had to be arranged in pleats. These fanned out over the hips from just below the waist where the side seams ended. The next step, which improved the fit and gave a better hang to the skirts, was to swing the back off the straight of the material and insert an extra pleat on either side of the centre back opening (*c.* 1720). The fronts also were slightly swung off the straight, and the side pleats often extended to take in all the available space possible. The sleeve, in keeping with the line of the coat, fitted to the elbow with a deep cuff coming over it, which was held in position by buttons; open sleeves had the outside of the cuff unstitched, but closed cuffs were more usual. This was the coat with 'full-dress'd' skirts as worn by the fashionable Beaux.

Having now reached its maximum fullness, from *c.* 1745 until the end of the century

the coat was gradually and gracefully to subside. The side seams, which were under the arms slightly towards the back while the coat was full, began to move further in to the centre back, and the shoulder-seam also dropped back. The fullness of the side pleats was reduced, the fronts straightened and then curved towards the sides. A narrow standing collar appeared *c.* 1760. The sleeves diminished in width but grew longer. By 1770 the narrow back (which by then had lost the extra centre back pleats) the fewer and shallower side pleats, the sloping front edges, the high standing collar and long sight sleeves with small fitting cuff, all contributed to produce the fashionable slender silhouette.

As well as these fashionable coats there were also simpler and more practical ones, made in cloth for outdoor wear. The country coat, while following the fashionable silhouette, was looser and simpler in cut. Single- or double-breasted, with a turned-down collar, it could be buttoned up for protection against inclement weather. This type of coat was called a frock and was increasingly worn from 1730 when the dress coat became so extravagant. In the last quarter of the century several innovations developed from the double-breasted frock. The top buttons were left undone so that the fronts which fell back formed revers; if worn on horseback the skirts were cut in horizontally at waist level to give them a better fall.

Unlike the French aristocracy, with their servile attendance at court, the English nobility spent a great part of the year on their country estates or visiting other country estates; always interested in sport, by the end of the eighteenth century it had become their all-absorbing occupation, and to riding, racing, and hunting had now been added driving. They spent so much of their lives in cloth, buckskin, and boots that by the 1780's their style of dress became fashionable wear and was only discarded for special occasions—Court attendance or a large 'rout'. In France too, influenced by Rousseau's teaching of a return to nature and simpler ways, a wave of Anglomania brought the English riding-coat to Paris, where, however, by incorporating some of its main features it was transformed into a fashionable silk version for the man of mode. The fronts of this coat were worn double-breasted with large revers and high collar; it also was cut across the waist, and the narrow front skirts, with one pleat only, were caught to the centre back panels, which by now had lost their side pleats—the cane had replaced the sword. The centre back was still slit open though there was usually an overlap of about an inch at the waist. The narrow skirts lengthened and became 'tails'. This was the introduction of the 'tail dress' coat for smart town wear. The earlier style with curved fronts and standing collar continued to be worn and was correct for Court and full dress; for informal wear it might have a turned-down collar. By 1790 full dress was only worn at Court.

Although the accepted length of all coats from 1680 onwards was to the knee, deviations can be seen. In the 1770's the eccentric 'Macaronis' preferred a long body with short tails, while the sporting 'Bucks' of the late 1780's favoured an exaggerated length of tails, especially when the coat was worn with the longer breeches and boots. A looser-fitting long coat, with the early wide back, was worn by the more conservative and older men until the end of the century. The coat of the working-man was much simpler in cut, with few or no pleats, wide unshaped back and many variations of length.

CAPES, GREAT-COATS

Capes were worn for travelling but became unfashionable by the middle of the century. A Roquelaure was a cape cut in three pieces, the side seams shaped to the shoulders. The great coat, or surtout, was a long loose overcoat, with just two side seams, slit up the centre back for riding, a standing or turned-down collar with sometimes a small cape as well. It was worn single- or double-breasted. When driving became the fashionable craze the sporting fraternity took over the coachman's great-coat with its multiple capes—the box coat. By the end of the century these great-coats were becoming fashionable town wear.

WAISTCOAT

The waistcoat worn with the early coats was cut on the same lines as the coat but always on the straight of the material, with less width in the skirts and no pleats. In the 1680's and 90's the waistcoat often had long sleeves which were seen below the shorter coat sleeves; later these were worn turned back over the coat cuff. In the early eighteenth century waistcoats with sleeves were often worn in the house, without a coat, otherwise they were sleeveless. When the front of the coat began to curve the waistcoat also curved, and became shorter. From the middle of the century variations in waistcoat styles were worn for undress. The most typical one was double-breasted with a small stand collar and it came just below waist level without basques. Waistcoats were always worn buttoned at the waist; often the top buttons were left undone to display the lace of the shirt. From the 80's double-breasted waistcoats with collars, revers, and no basques were informal wear with all types of coats.

BREECHES

By 1690 the breeches had lost all their superfluous trimmings though they were still cut rather full. In the early eighteenth century they were still ample in the seat; usually they fitted over the knee but the man of mode might have them shorter when he wore his stockings rolled. Rolled stockings were the fade-out of the old boot hose. The wide tops gradually shrank and became cuffs which fitted over the knee, a fashion which lingered on until the 1740's. The breeches were almost hidden under the long coat, waistcoat and rolled stockings so that they were cut more for comfort than fit. From the second half of the century, with the fronts of the coat cut away and the shorter waistcoat, much more of the breeches were shown, and consequently they became more fitted to the thigh and over the knee; *c.* 1770 for undress wear bunches of laces often replaced the knee buckle. From *c.* 1750 also the centre front fly was replaced by 'falls' —a flap opening. Backs were still cut full. The long-tailed coats of the 1790's demanded even tighter-fitting breeches, and as well as being cut in buckskin they were sometimes cut on the cross from jersey-weave materials. For day wear with boots the legs were extended well below the knee and eventually to the calves. This type was called 'pantaloons' to distinguish them from knee breeches.

MATERIALS, DECORATION

The coat on its first appearance for fashionable wear was barely visible under its fungus of ribbon and lace, waist sash and wide baldrick. The straight coat of the 1680's and 90's might still have the sash and baldrick, either worn together or separately, but now its main feature was the braid or gold or silver lace trimmings. These often covered all the seams, as well as centre fronts, edges of centre backs and side skirts. There was also a great variety of pocket shapes, their decoration being repeated on the cuffs, but *c.* 1700 pockets became conventional and varied little throughout the eighteenth century. They had scalloped flaps and were always set on a level with the top of the side pleats.

The seventeenth-century coat retained the buttons and buttonholes down centre fronts, centre back and side openings, as seen in the original casaque. When *c.* 1700 the sides were set in pleats one button only was kept at the top of the pleats. Front button-holes from the waist down were sham, as were also the back buttonholes, and these purely decorative buttonholes were discarded from the middle of the century. From the 1690's onwards the tendency was to wear the coat unbuttoned, or only fastened at the waist. By 1770 the embroidered full dress coat often dispensed with buttonholes altogether, though the buttons stayed as decoration. These coats could be fastened by hooks and eyes across the chest.

Encouraged by Louis XIV and his astute minister, Colbert, the French by the end of the seventeenth century had taken the lead in the manufacture of silks, brocades, damasks, velvets, etc., as well as gold and silver braids, lace and all the other luxury accessories to dress. The arrival in England of many French immigrant silk weavers, after the revocation of the Edict of Nantes 1685, gave great impetus to the small silk industry which their compatriots had established in Spitalfields a hundred years earlier. These French and English silks were so beautiful that decoration became unnecessary. The full-skirted 1720–50 coat, which owed its style to cut, was often untrimmed and worn with matching untrimmed waistcoat and breeches. Stiff figured silks with a small all-over design were specially woven for these suits. Earlier and later, contrasting waist-coats of richer material were worn, though the breeches usually matched the coat. Full dress and Court suits were much more elaborate, either heavily embroidered with gold, silver and colours, or decorated with wide gold or silver lace, later also sequins. After 1750, except for Court dress, the fashion of edging all seams with braid was relegated to military and livery suits. The application of decoration on all eighteenth-century coats became very conservative—down the centre fronts, centre backs from waist, pockets and round the pockets, and on the cuffs. From 1730–60 this decoration was woven in position on coat lengths. The decoration always echoed the ornamental style of its period and was admirably suited to each succeeding change of line. The stiff heavy Baroque patterns of the late seventeenth century changed to the softer rounded forms of the Rococco, and then thinned out to the delicate fine-spun lines of the last quarter of the century. The designs of brocades and other patterned silks followed the same pro-cess—large bold shapes diminished to tiny spots and broad stripes narrowed down to thin lines. The Baroque colours were rich and heavy, the Rococco clear and flower-like, with the brilliance that only vegetable dyes can give. By the end of the cen-tury the colours were muted—the famous *puce, cheveux de la Reine, boue de Paris*, etc.

Sometimes the only decoration on a coat was the ornamental buttonholes and button placings—across the fronts, on the pockets and sleeves and down the centre back vent. These were called 'froggings' or 'Brandenbourgs', and probably originated from the braided fastenings of the Eastern European kaftans. They were made from cords, braids, little tassels and spangles, gold or silver, or in colours to match the coat.

Cloth was always as much worn as silk, even for Court dress, when it would be of superfine quality and always heavily embroidered. For informal wear the Englishman favoured cloth, with just a narrow gold or silver braid edging to the fronts, pockets, etc. The frock might be similarly trimmed.

By the end of the century only the full dress Court suits were decorated. Many variations of trimming and styles of revers, cuffs, etc., which cropped up and faded out were, however, retained to become the glory of military uniform for many years to come.

CONSTRUCTION OF THE EIGHTEENTH-CENTURY COAT

All eighteenth-century coats have the top of the centre back vents, side pleatings of the skirts and the pocket line on the same level round the body (this varies a little in height); the seams of the coat are stitched down to this level. The front and back side fullness, when pleated, is firmly stitched together inside at the top and then only caught at the bottom where there is often a button. The narrower and longer skirts of the 1780's and 90's are caught in several places. The necks of the early collarless coats are usually finished with a half-inch band tapering off to nothing. The fit on the shoulders and round the armholes is awkward to a modern eye as there is rarely any padding or interlining unless some physical defect has to be disguised. The only body padding is on the front from the collar-bone down to the chest.

All eighteenth-century coats have the full length of the centre front edges and centre back skirts strengthened with a firm strip of linen, or buckram, about four inches wide. A small piece of firm linen, sometimes backed with paper, is attached to the top of the side pleats and top of back slits. Until *c.* 1760 the very full coats have the front skirts, from the pockets down, interlined with linen or buckram, which is often covered with a thin layer of teased-out horsehair. The pleats of this coat are also interlined with a thin woollen material or teased-out wool fibres—this is lightly caught to the silk lining (there is no other interlining). (Diagram XXXIV. For variations in arranging the extra centre back pleats, 1720–70, see Diagrams XVIII, XIX, XX, XXI.)

In the second half of the century interlining in the skirts and pleats is very rare.

All coats, except great-coats, are lined, usually with silk. In cloth coats all edges are cut and left raw.

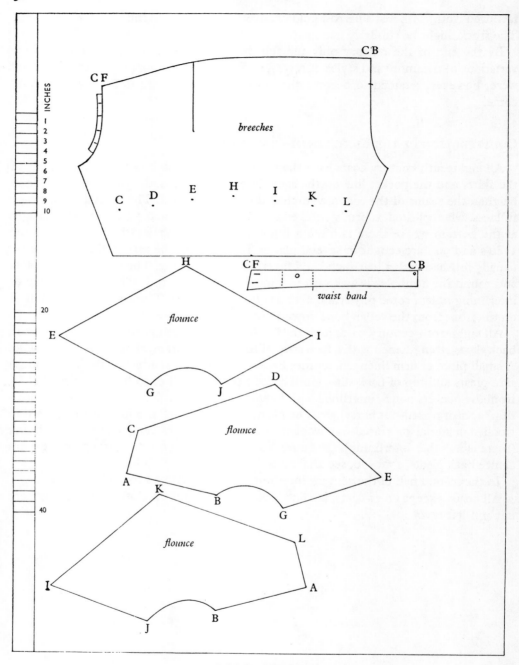

INCHES
1
2
3
4
5
6
7
8
9
10

20

40

DIAGRAM XV

COAT AND BREECHES 1681. White brocade with small sprigs in gold thread. The button-holes are worked in gold. The sleeves and cuffs are cut in one and turned back on the dotted line. The cuffs are faced with pink brocade. Lined cream silk. The flounce on the breeches is sewn round the bottom of the leg and turned back and caught to the breeches at C, D, E, H, I, K, L. *Victoria and Albert Museum*

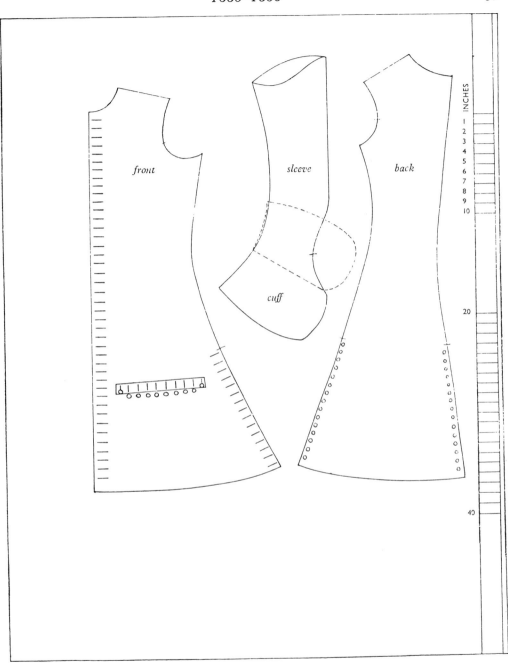

DIAGRAM XV

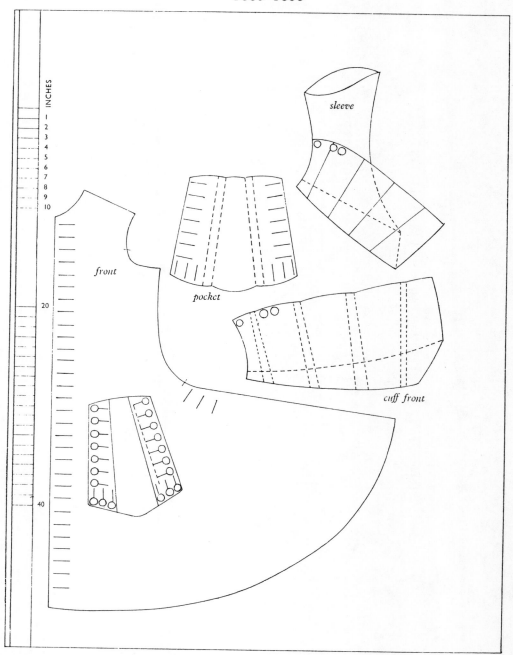

DIAGRAM XVI

COAT AND BREECHES *c.* 1680–90. Brown wool. The pockets and cuffs of the same material as the coat are arranged in flat pleats as indicated by the dotted lines. Basket-weave buttons. The last eight button-holes are false. Blue-brown shot-silk lining. A two-inch belt of blue brocade is attached inside to the side seams at waist; with silver fringe. (The breeches are from a 1670 suit.) *The Gallery of Costume, Manchester*

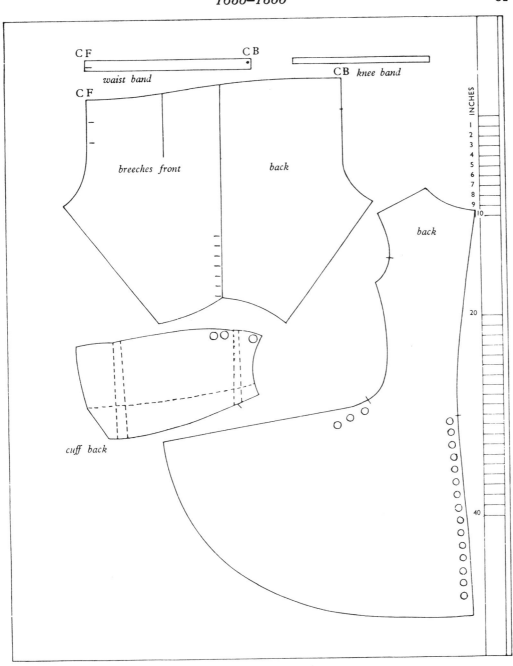

CF CB
waist band

CB *knee band*

CF

breeches front

back

back

cuff back

INCHES
1
2
3
4
5
6
7
8
9
10
20
40

DIAGRAM XVI

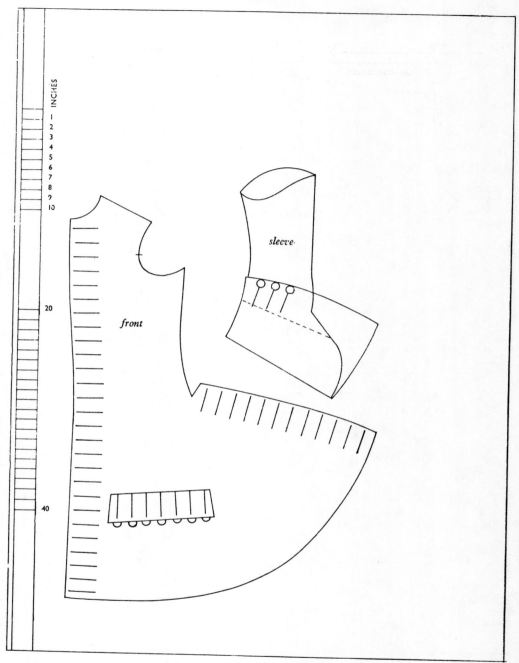

INCHES
1
2
3
4
5
6
7
8
9
10

20

40

sleeve

front

DIAGRAM XVII

COAT *c.* 1700. Mauve-grey cloth. All edges are cut, but the neck has a quarter-inch binding of self. The button-holes are worked in silver thread to match the silver-thread basket-weave buttons. The back button-holes, as also the side skirt button-holes (except the top one, worn buttoned), are false. Lined grey silk. This is a simple day coat; usually now the side skirts are set in pleats. *Victoria and Albert Museum*

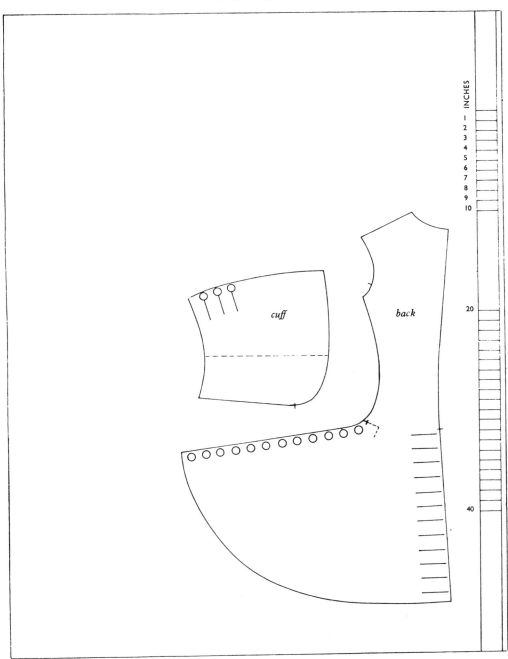

cuff

back

INCHES
1
2
3
4
5
6
7
8
9
10

20

40

DIAGRAM XVII

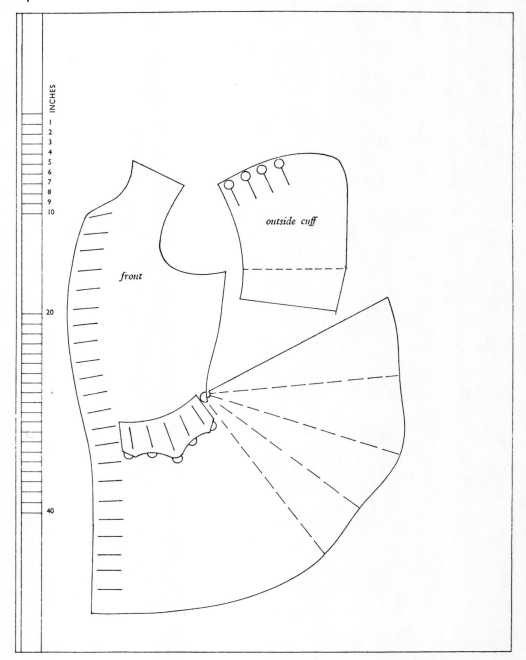

INCHES

1
2
3
4
5
6
7
8
9
10

20

40

front

outside cuff

DIAGRAM XVIII

COAT *c.* 1720–7. Heavy fawn silk. Button-holes worked in darker fawn silk to match basket-weave buttons. The last eight, also the back, button-holes are false. The deep cuff comes over the elbow and the back seam is open from X. Lined silk in a lighter shade. *Victoria and Albert Museum*

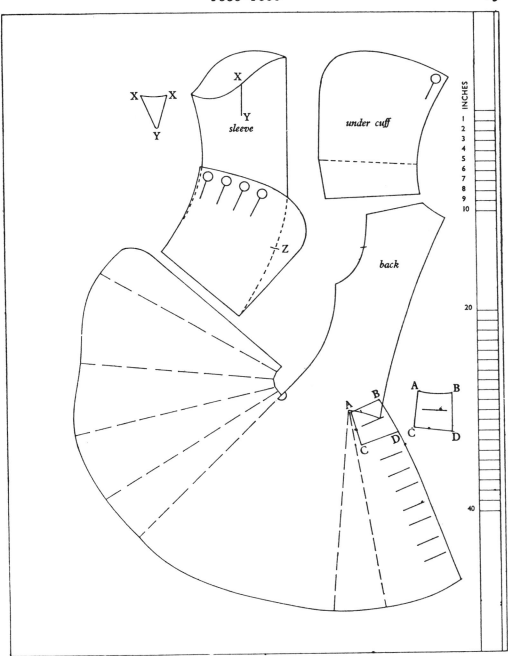

DIAGRAM XVIII

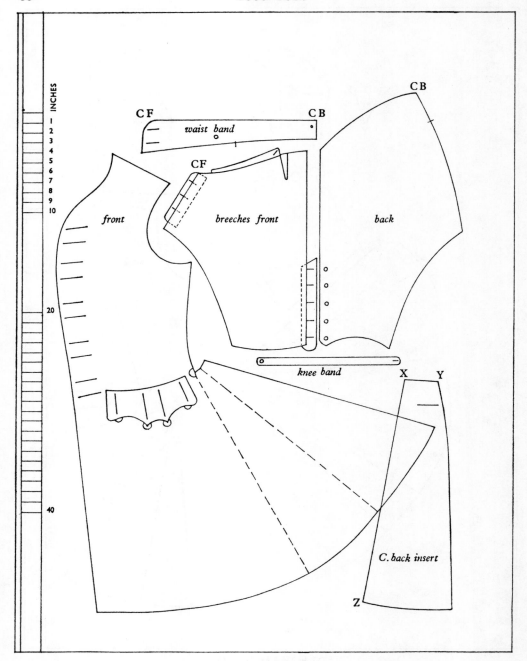

DIAGRAM XIX

COAT AND BREECHES *c.* 1730. Brown wool shot yellow. Button-holes worked in dark brown silk to match the basket-weave buttons. The top button-hole and the last four work, the rest are false. Bright yellow silk lining to coat, breeches lined chamois leather. *London Museum*

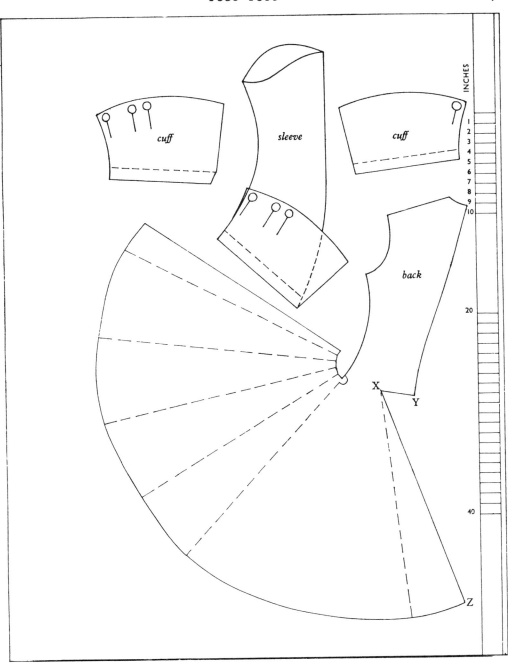

INCHES

cuff

sleeve

cuff

back

X
Y

Z

1
2
3
4
5
6
7
8
9
10

20

40

DIAGRAM XIX

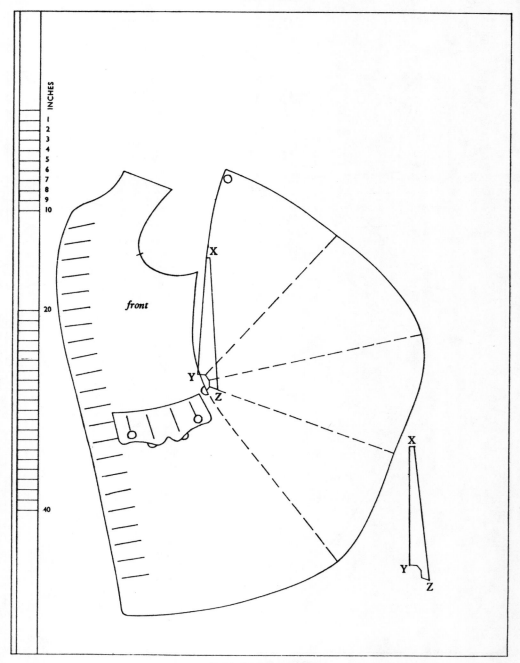

INCHES
1 2 3 4 5 6 7 8 9 10 20 40

front

X
Y
Z

X
Y
Z

DIAGRAM XX

COAT *c.* 1735–40 (see plate 11). Stiff figured cream silk with small all-over pattern in fawns and brown. The last eight button-holes, as also the back ones, are false. Button-holes worked in cream silk to match basket-weave buttons. Cream silk lining. This is the most extravagant cut for an eighteenth-century coat and this one is probably of French origin. Similar coats have matching waistcoat and breeches. *Gallery of Costume, Manchester*

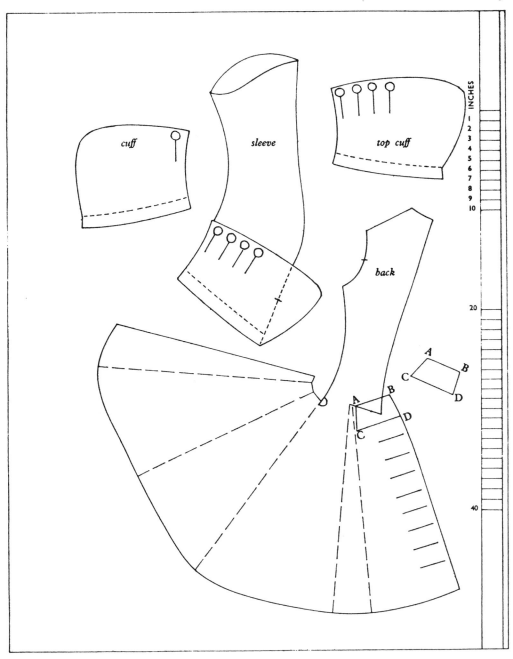

DIAGRAM XX

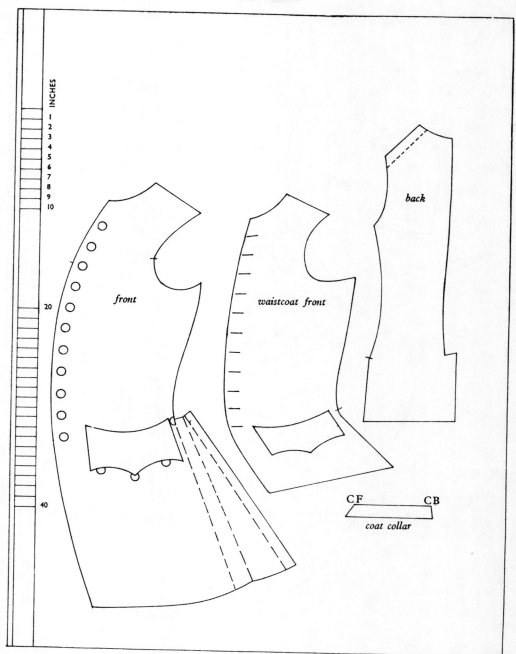

DIAGRAM XXI

COAT, WAISTCOAT, AND BREECHES *c.* 1760. Rose-coloured silk with narrow self stripe, embroidered in coloured tambour work down centre fronts, centre back slits, side skirts, pockets and cuffs. Flat buttons embroidered to match, no button-holes, hooks on chest. The waistcoat is embroidered to match, the back is of holland. *Victoria and Albert Museum*

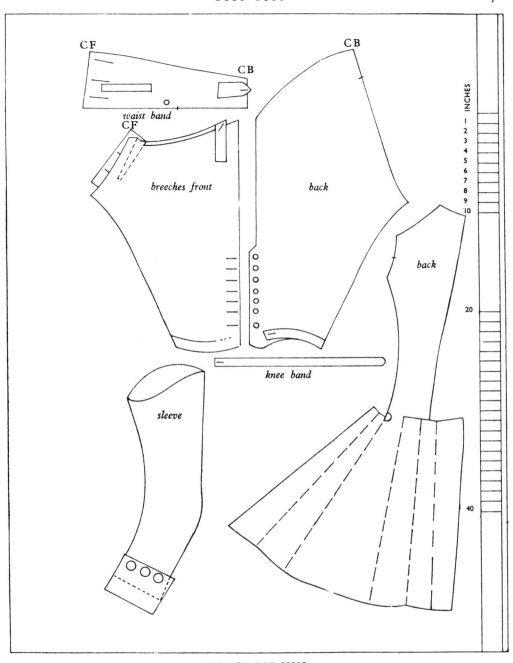

CF

CB

CB

waist band

CF

breeches front

back

back

knee band

sleeve

DIAGRAM XXI

INCHES

1
2
3
4
5
6
7
8
9
10

20

40

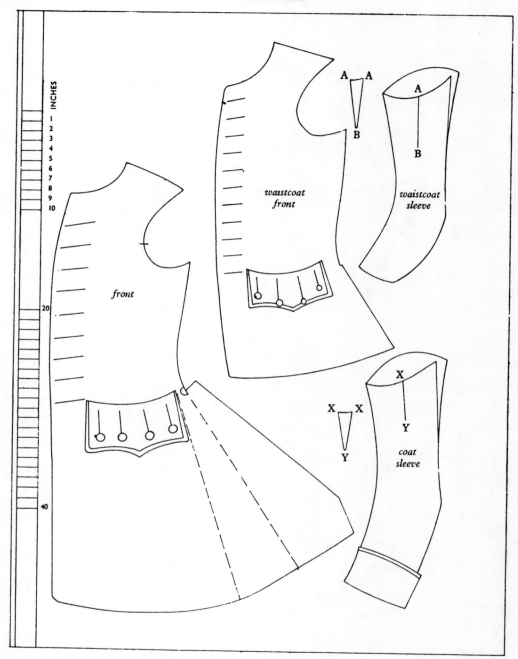

INCHES
1 2 3 4 5 6 7 8 9 10
20
40

waistcoat front

waistcoat sleeve

A A
B

A
B

front

X X
Y

X
Y

coat sleeve

DIAGRAM XXII

FROCK, WAISTCOAT, AND BREECHES *c. 1760–5*. Mauve-grey cloth. The edges are cut and the fronts and centre back slits are edged with one row silver cord, the collar, pockets and cuffs have two rows. The collar is faced with fawn velvet and can be worn either turned down or buttoned up. All the button-holes work and the buttons are engraved steel. The knees of the breeches are slotted to take a ribbon tie. Cloth suits of this simpler cut were worn for travelling or in the country. *Gallery of Costume, Manchester*

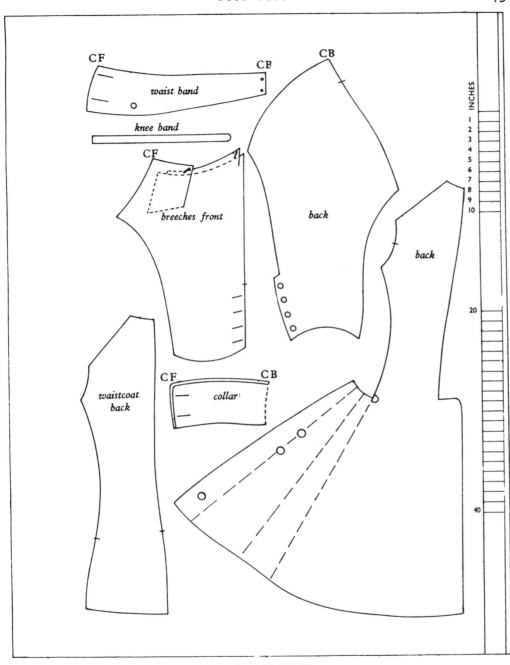

DIAGRAM XXII

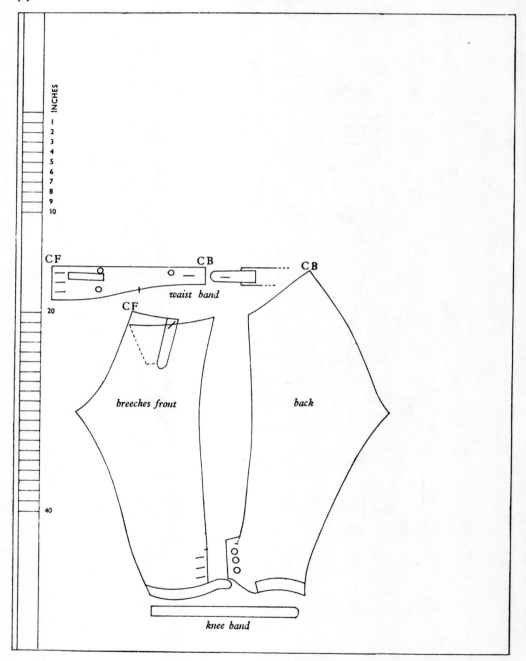

INCHES

1
2
3
4
5
6
7
8
9
10

CF   CB   CB
waist band

20

CF

breeches front   *back*

40

knee band

DIAGRAM XXIII

COAT AND BREECHES *c.* 1775 (see plate 14a). Light tobacco brown silk with self satin stripe, beautifully embroidered in colours in a delicate floral design down centre fronts, centre back slits, bottom side skirts, collar, pockets and cuffs, also flat buttons and knee bands to breeches—no button-holes, hooks on chest. This is a full-dress suit and would be worn with an embroidered white silk or satin waistcoat. *Victoria and Albert Museum*

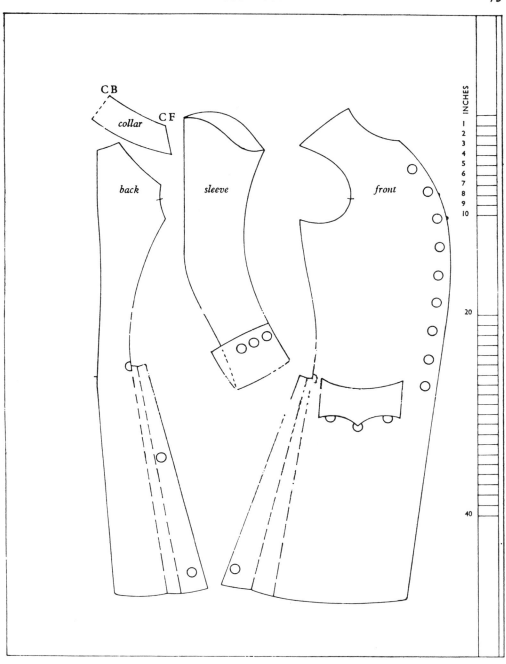

CB

collar

CF

back

sleeve

front

INCHES

1
2
3
4
5
6
7
8
9
10

20

40

DIAGRAM XXIII

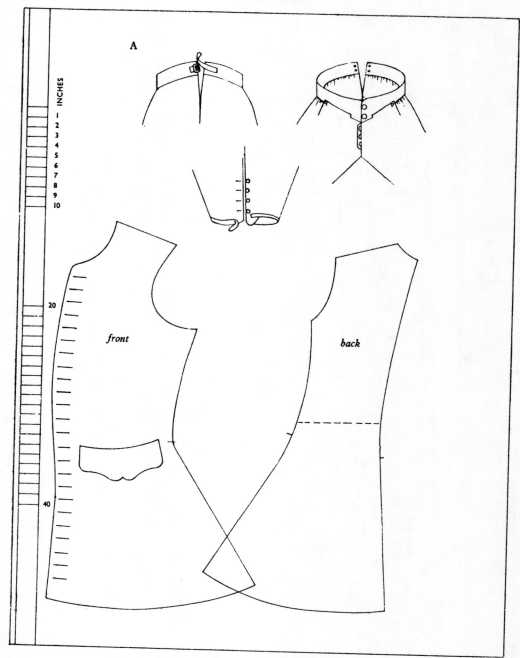

DIAGRAM XXIV

WAISTCOAT *c.* 1715–25. Rose-coloured silk, embroidered in same coloured silk down centre fronts and pockets. The back body is of holland but the back skirts of the silk. *London Museum*

A. Detail of breeches with centre front opening, as usual until *c.* 1770.

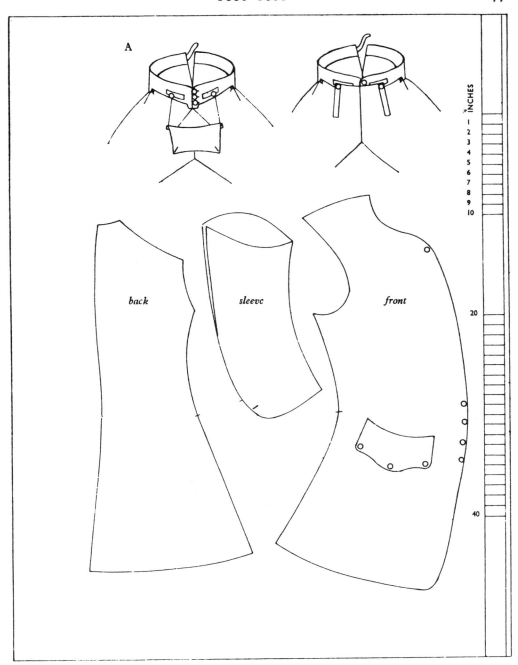

INCHES
1
2
3
4
5
6
7
8
9
10

20

40

back

sleeve

front

A

DIAGRAM XXV

WAISTCOAT WITH SLEEVES 1720–40. White satin heavily embroidered down fronts and pockets in gold and coloured silks. *Museum für Angewandte Kunst, Vienna*

A. Detail of breeches with flap opening, as worn from 1770 onwards.

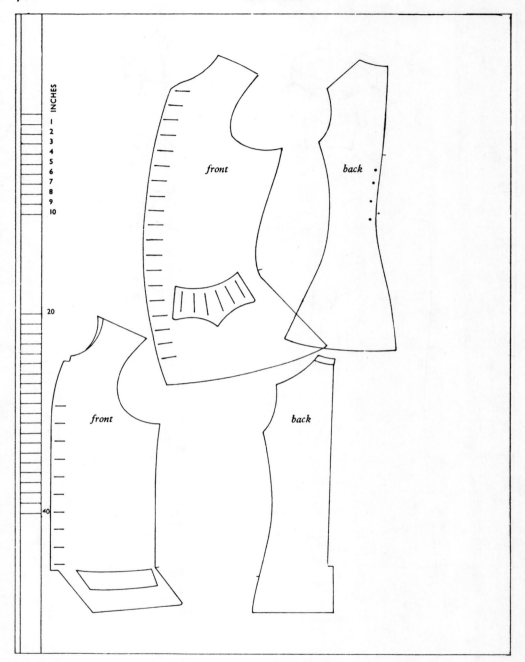

DIAGRAM XXVI

WAISTCOAT *c.* 1735–40. Stiff figured cream silk with an all-over small design in fawns and claret. The back is also of the same silk and stitched at the top and then laces. No trimming. Worn with coat similar to Diagram XX. *Victoria and Albert Museum*

DIAGRAM XXVII

WAISTCOAT *c.* 1770. Pale cream silk, lightly embroidered centre fronts and pockets. The back is of holland. *Private Collection*

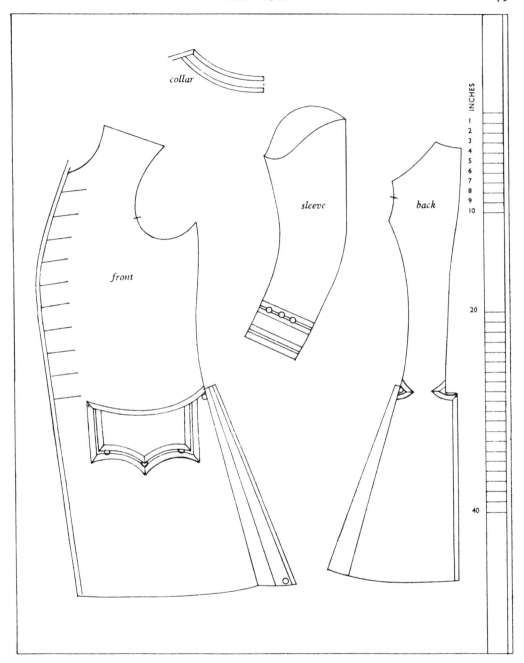

collar

sleeve

front

back

INCHES
1
2
3
4
5
6
7
8
9
10

20

40

DIAGRAM XXVIII

COAT 1770–80's. Tan cloth trimmed silver braid—steel buttons. A typical day coat of the last quarter of the century. *Victoria and Albert Museum*

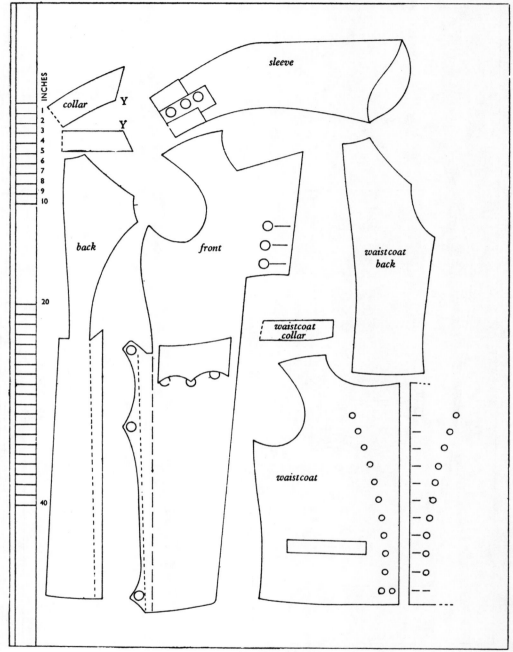

DIAGRAM XXIX

COAT AND WAISTCOAT *c.* 1790. Stiff silk in narrow yellow, black and white stripes. The side pleats are attached to the back panel by the buttons which are of steel. The waistcoat is of white silk with narrow horizontal stripes in black. (The sleeve should be cut on the vertical straight.) *Victoria and Albert Museum*

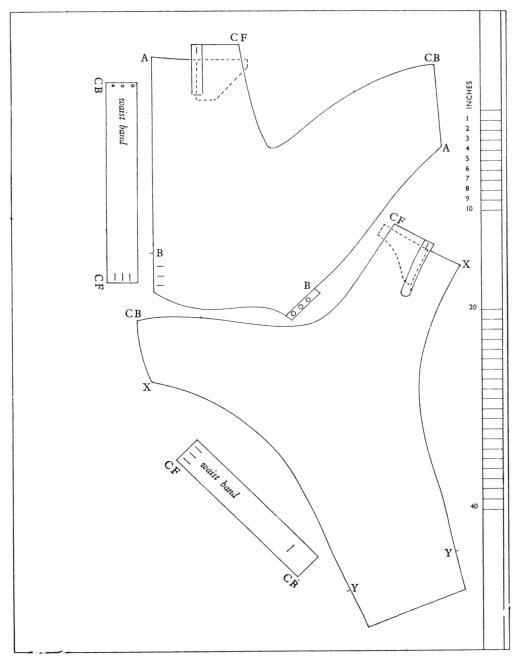

DIAGRAM XXX

BREECHES *c.* 1780. Black silk jersey. These breeches are cut with only outside leg seams. There is a slot round the knee to take a ribbon tie. *Victoria and Albert Museum*

DIAGRAM XXXI

PANTALOONS *c.* 1795. Heavy white jersey-weave cotton. Only one leg seam on the outside. *Victoria and Albert Museum*

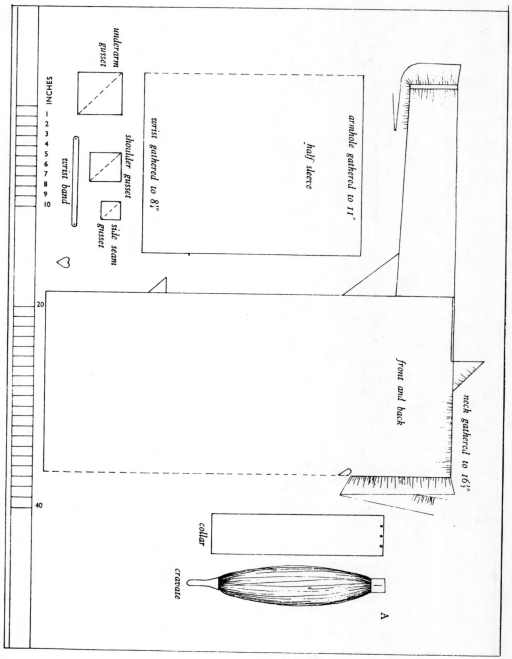

underarm
gusset

shoulder gusset

wrist band

wrist gathered to 8⅞″

side seam
gusset

half sleeve

armhole gathered to 11″

20

front and back

neck gathered to 16⅜″

40

collar

cravate

A

DIAGRAM XXXII

SHIRT 1700–1810. The centre front opening is usually trimmed with a frill of lace or, at the end of the period, fine lawn. The wrist frill is often mounted separately but is rare after 1800. *Gallery of Costume, Manchester*

A. CRAVATE. From *c.* 1720 the cravate was shortened to fit round the neck where it was fastened by tapes, buttons or a buckle.

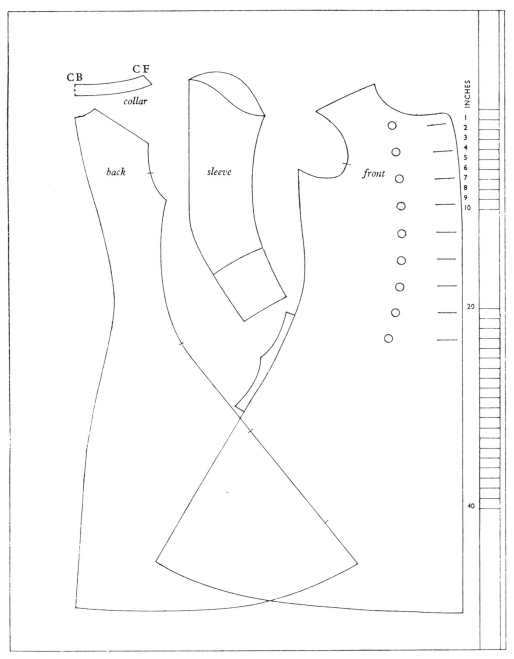

DIAGRAM XXXIII

DRESSING-GOWN *c.* 1750. Blue silk damask. Double-breasted and seamed all down centre back and side seams to within a few inches of the bottom—pocket in side seam. Button-holes and matching basket-weave buttons in blue silk. The fronts and back are lined with wool down to the level of the bottom button-hole. A matching waistcoat is similar to Diagram XXVI. *Gallery of Costume, Manchester*

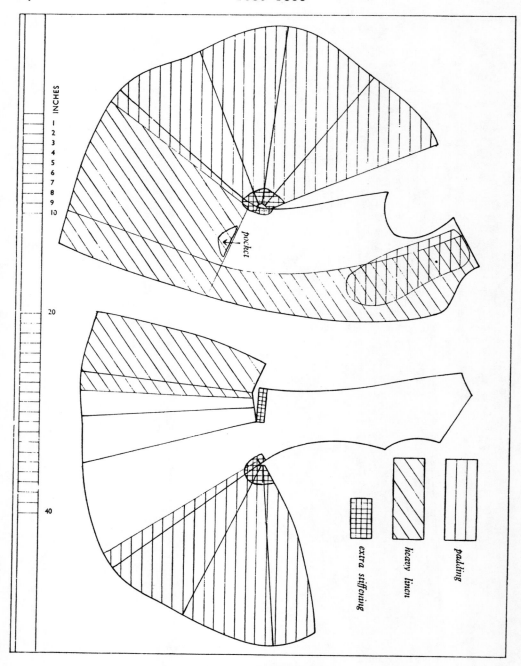

INCHES

1
2
3
4
5
6
7
8
9
10

20

40

pocket

extra stiffening

heavy linen

padding

DIAGRAM XXXIV

CONSTRUCTION OF COAT. In the second half of the century the skirt and pleat interlinings
are omitted but the centre front, centre back skirt and extra top pleat stiffening retained.

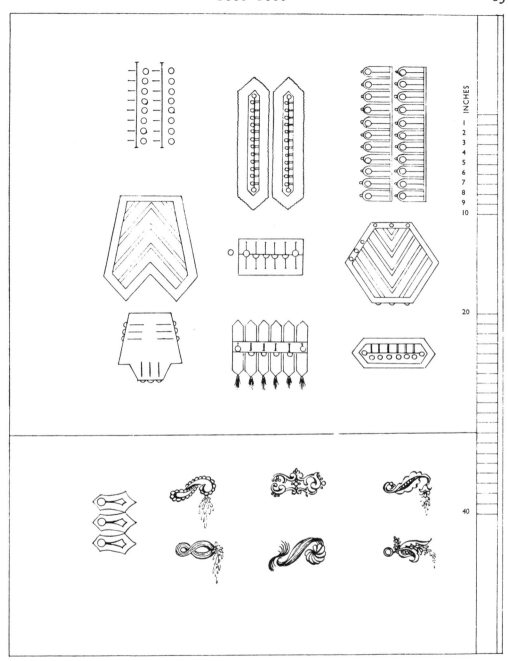

DIAGRAM XXXV

POCKETS 1680–90. These variations of pocket styles are usually carried out in flat braids or gold or silver lace, the same design usually being repeated on the cuffs.

DIAGRAM XXXVI

FROGGINGS *c.* 1750–80's. These are an ornate design for button-holes and button placings and are made from fancy braids, cords, tassels, etc., often mixed with gold or silver metal threads and foil, spangles and sequins. On simpler coats the froggings are the same colour as the coat itself.

Eighteenth-century Tailoring

———◦•❖◦❋◦❖•◦———

The first really serious treatise on the art of tailoring, *L'Art du Tailleur*, was written by M. de Garsault for the encyclopaedia, *Description des Arts et Métiers*, published by the Académie Royale des Sciences, Paris, 1769. He describes the whole process of making a coat, from taking the measurements to a detailed account of the making—the stitches used, method of·pressing, instruments required, etc. The text is accompanied by plates —the diagrams of patterns given illustrate the garments mentioned in the text and show how to place them on material. There is still no mention of fitting, although in the section on Corset Making (tailors also made women's corsets, which was a specialized branch of the trade) M. de Garsault gives instructions for fitting before the corset is completed.

Several other encyclopaedias were published in France during the second half of the eighteenth century, the section on tailoring being always based on M. de Garsault's text and plates. The best known is Diderot's *Encyclopaedia*, 1771. Here again the text is from M. de Garsault, but small details of construction have been eliminated and others brought up to date.

The following extracts, somewhat condensed, from M. de Garsault's 1769 text, illustrate eighteenth-century methods of tailoring:

MEASUREMENTS

First the tailor must take the measurements of the person for whom the clothes are going to be made; a strip of paper, one inch wide and of the requisite length, is used, it is called a measure. It is placed on the body wherever the size is required and each measurement is marked on the measure by a snip of the scissors. The tailor should take note of the physique of his customer—high or sloping shoulders, shape and size of stomach, flat or pigeon-chested, etc., so as to cut accordingly; if the customer has some physical defect it should be noted so as to be skilfully disguised with extra stiffening, padding, etc.

Measurements Required

a, round the arm	m, length to coat pocket
b, breadth of back	n, length of waistcoat
c, breadth of front	o, length of coat, back
d, length of arm to elbow	p, length of coat, front
e, length of arm	q, round the knee
f, round the body at waist	r, round the middle of the thigh
g, round the body above waist	s, round the top of the thigh
h, round the body below waist	t, round the waist
i, length to waist	u, length of breeches
l, length to waistcoat pocket	

The waistcoat should be measured as for the coat, but taken tighter.

Cutting-out

The material to be used is spread on the cutting table and folded double, lengthwise (if the material is narrow two lengths are used). The tailor draws his shapes on the top layer and the two thicknesses are cut out together.

The tailor should have several paper patterns of different sizes as they are a great help in drawing out his garments—these need only be to the length of the pocket. When he has chosen a pattern which is the approximate size of his measurements, he places it on the material and draws it lightly with chalk, he checks this with his measurements, marks them and then draws through these points the body of the coat. He should also have patterns for sleeves, cuffs, waistcoat, breeches, etc. After the complete suit—coat, waistcoat, breeches—has been drawn the tailor cuts them out, but before doing this he must make sure that all the pieces are arranged so as to leave as little waste material as possible.

Construction

The very first step must be to strengthen the top of the side pleats, both fronts and backs, as they could easily be split while the coat is being made. The strengthening is done by adding a piece of firm material (*droit-fil*), the shape of an inverted horse-shoe, to the reverse side, and it is caught to the coat along the pocket line, as the stitching will be hidden when the pocket flap is added. Next the centre back pleat has to be arranged —when the material has been folded to form a pleat it will be seen that there is a gap between the body of the coat and the skirt, and this gap must be filled in by a small square of material (*cran*), this square will be disguised when the buttonholes are worked over the joins. If there is a border and no buttonholes the tailor must be very skilful in making his pleat so that there is no gap.

The fronts must then be stiffened with buckram. It is tacked to the reverse side from top to bottom along the edges, four inches broad at the shoulders, widening to within two inches at the armhole, then narrowing to the seventh or eighth buttonhole where it continues straight to the bottom, just a little wider than the buttonholes. The tailor then marks the buttonholes, they are usually two or two and a half inches long and two inches apart for the coat, and one and a half inches for the waistcoat.

When the buttonholes have been worked a second piece of buckram is added the same size as the first but only the length of the seventh or eighth buttonhole. Then a strip of straight material (*droit-fil*) is placed all along the edge, pleated to shape where the chest is rounded, and all three layers of stiffening are then whip-stitched to the edge of the coat. A small plastron of cotton wool is stitched to the buckram on the chest towards the collar-bone to fill in the hollow which is always found there.

The pocket holes are then cut, the pockets attached inside, and the flaps stitched over them outside.

The skirt of the coat used to have a horsehair (*crin*) lining to hold it out, and was called a 'pannier'—some customers still like a little pannier, the horsehair coming only half-way down the skirt ('Panniers are no longer fashionable.' 1771).

The backs are joined together by backstitching on the wrong side and then fine-drawing on the right, working from the skirt opening upwards. The centre back at the opening is strengthened by a strip of straight material (*droit-fil*). Before sewing the fronts to the backs, pin them together and check by the measurements. Sew the armhole down to where the pleats begin, then sew the shoulder seams, using in each case the same stitches as for the centre back join. Place the neck edging—this is a straight fold of material—one inch wide narrowing at either end.

Make the side pleats, folding first above, then below—four pleats in the front, and two and a half in the back.

Catch the bottom of the side pleats together with a couple of stitches, and all pleats together at the top, using a strong thread double.

Make the sleeves and attach them.

The waistcoat is made in the same way but has only one buckram interlining which does not go as far as the shoulder.

PRESSING

The art of the tailor consists above all in cutting and pressing—the latter process giving the garment the elegant durable shape it should have. This operation, which is very delicate, is sufficient in itself to give a garment a good or bad shape, according to the way in which it is executed, for it can spoil one which has been well cut out and improve another whose cut had been imperfect.

OTHER TYPES OF GARMENTS

The *Surtout* is a country coat but now worn in town. The only difference is that the buttonholes stop at pocket level and there are only three buttonholes on the centre back vent. Usually with a collar.

The *Volant* is also a coat, but has no buttonholes or buttons on the sleeves, no pocket flaps, it laps over centre back and has a collar with button and buttonhole; it is usually worn over the coat.

The *Fraque* is also a coat of recent fashion; it has few pleats and no pocket flaps.

All these three coats are made like the coat.

The *Redingotte* is a recent fashion imported from England and is like its English name, a riding coat. It is a cloak with sleeves, and buttons to the waist. It has a collar like the *Surtout* and the back of the neck is arranged in pleats which are hidden by a cape collar (*rotonne*). The sleeves have boot cuffs with three buttons and buttonholes and are lined with linen. The fronts are lined to the waist with the same material. There are sometimes pockets on the side seams. The centre back opening is only half as high as that of the coat. It is made from cloth or similar stout material.

The *Roquelaure*, named after the original wearer, is very useful for travelling or riding. It has buttons and buttonholes at the neck and is usually made in cloth.

The *Manteau* is the old circular cloak which is now out of fashion but may come in again as it gives good protection against cold weather when worn on foot or horseback. It is seamed up the centre back with an opening like the *Redingotte*, and it also is pleated round the neck with a cape collar. No lining except for a band of itself each side centre front. It has no buttons but a hook at the neck. Usually made in cloth it is from three to five inches longer than the coat.

The *Soutanelle* is the coat worn by the clergy. It buttons all up the front with very small buttons, there is no centre back opening and only four pleats at the side.

The *Soutane* is the long robe worn by the clergy. It fits like the coat, then widens and reaches to the ground. It is always made from black cloth and is interlined with black linen instead of buckram. There is a six-inch opening on the side seam at the hips, and above that is a cord to hold the sash which is made from black silk ribbon four inches wide with long ends. It buttons from neck to hem with very small buttons.

The *Robe de Chambre* is made in two styles. The one with separate sleeves is made like the *Soutane*. It has a collar with button and buttonhole, and sometimes buttons to the waist. The other style *en chemise*—the sleeves cut with the body—is made like the first, but pieces have to be added to give length to the sleeves.

The *Veston* is a new-fashioned waistcoat with very short basques and narrow pocket, worn under the *Redingotte*.

The *Camisole* or *Gilet* is worn next the skin (flannel), or over the shirt (various materials). It is made like the waistcoat, with or without sleeves. It is unlined but faced down the fronts, and buttons with very small flat buttons (pages 93, 94, 95).

FRENCH TERMS USED WITH THE ENGLISH EQUIVALENT

Justaucorps } *Surtout* }	— Coat
Fraque } *Volant* }	— Frock
Redingotte	— Great coat, cape coat, surtout
Manteau	— Circular cloak
Roquelaure	— Roquelaure
Veste } *Veston* }	— Waistcoat, vest
Camisole } *Gilet* }	— Underwaistcoat, camisol
Robe de Chambre	— Night gown, or morning gown
Culotte	— Breeches
Habit	— Suit
Soutanelle	— Short cassock
Soutane	— Cassock
Bougran	— Buckram, made from old sheets, or linen stiffened with size
Chanteau	— Piece added when material is not wide enough
Cran	— Small piece of material added to fill a gap
Droit-fil	— Band of strong linen used for strengthening.

In England also many encyclopaedias appeared during the eighteenth century, but none of them with such a comprehensive description of tailoring as that of Garsault. *A General Description of All Trades, digested in Alphabetical Order*, London, 1747, however, contains some useful information:

BUCKRAM-STIFFENERS

'Their Business is, by often wetting, with a sort of glutinous Matter, prepared by themselves, and as often drying, so to order all sorts of Linnen-cloth, as to render it of several Degrees of Stiffness, which, together with the Calenders Work, converts it into what is called Buckram, the Article that makes so considerable a Figure in every Taylor's Bill.'

BUTTON-MAKERS

'These are of two Kinds: the one, who cover the Moulds with divers Sortes of Twists, etc. in many curious Mixtures and Shapes, on which Women work; The other, who make Buttons of all the different Metals after various Methods; every one keeping to his own branch; many of late are made of fine Stones, etc., but these are altogether Men's Employ.'

Taylors

'The most general Use of Cloathing makes the Experience of their Commodiousness almost universal, the Inhabitants of above three Parts of the known World, having come to the knowledge of it; but with respect to the Variety, and often changing the Mode or Fashion, none come up to France and England.

'As to the working Part one would think, by looking on, it is easy, but it will tire a stout man that follows it all Day closely, and it requires very good Eye-sight and a quick Hand to make good Wages at it which most of them do, and the least they are allowed by Act of Parliament is 1s. 10d. a Day. But the most dextrous Part is cutting-out, on which depends the Fitting and Shape, the principal Articles that give Ease and Pleasure to the Wearers, and obtain Customers; therefore, a Man is not properly qualified to set up for himself who has not got a pretty good knack at it.

'Some Masters carry a great Business indeed, many of them in a middling Way live exceedingly handsome, and the honest Class of them that are frugal get a good Livelihood, and some of the first Sort have left Estates behind them.

'They take with an Apprentice 5 or 10 l. whose working Hours are from six to eight; and he may set up as a Master, when out of his Time, very well with 100 l. but some employ many Hundreds.'

The earliest known English book on tailoring is *The Taylor's Complete Guide, or a Comprehensive Analysis of Beauty and Elegance in Dress . . . Illustrated by Copper Plates . . . The whole Concentrated and Devised by a Society of Adepts in the Profession*, London, 1796. This work gives a slightly new approach to cutting as the tailor is instructed how to draw his coat on to material by using his measurements and following the Diagrams given in the plates. There is also a section on alterations.

'As we write for the inexperienced and uninformed, it may not be amiss for us to define and lay down a certain rule that may be a lasting standard for all such as are unacquainted with the real quantity of cloth necessary to make a coat; take the following method:—Measure by your yard the length of your coat, as you have taken from your measure, to which add the length of your sleeve, these two added together will be the precise quantity requisite, and no less will do with any propriety.

'When the cloth is laid before you, do not omit to have recourse to the plate of the analysis of coats, and pay particular respect to the separated parts, the different modes and turnings that they effect, for until these are made (as it were) coincident with your own ideas, the maxims we lay down, we are fearful, will only serve to confuse, without answering the great end we wish to obtain by our labours. After you have sufficiently digested the plates, and your cloth being before you, mark down the back seam, as the plate directs, and strike the shape of the back upon the cloth, bearing the same similitude as the plate, and take care it answers to your measure in every part. Take a large back hollowing, for this will make your back skirts lap over well and not part behind, as is too often the case, to the abuse of decency.'

This book is also interesting because it has a 'description how to cut out and make the patent elastic Habits and Cloaths without the usual seams, now in the highest estimation with the Nobility and Gentry, according to a patent granted by his Majesty'. Although this method is given for body garments and sleeves its real success must have been when used to cut the fashionable tight-fitting pantaloons and breeches.

'Cutting and making Worsted Stocking-breeches, ribbed or plain.

'When at your cutting board and have your stocking-piece before you, observe the following maxim, which entirely results from the stretch or elasticity that there is in all framework of this nature, and requires that the breeches must be three inches longer than the measure. But for more particulars we refer to the Plates.

'Lay your measure upon the piece within one inch and a half of the top, then extend it to the intended place for the knee, and mark it and cut it longer an inch and a half below at the knee; then for the width, lay on the measure at the bottom of the knee, and mark for cutting one inch narrower than the measure upon the stuff in the double, and one inch less in gradation all the way up the thigh, and be sure to abide by the following example for the stride:—First make a deep fall down, and having laid your finger upon the measure at the bottom of the knee, with the other hand extend the measure to the fork, and make the stride within three inches of the length of the measure, this will give proper room for the elasticity of the materials, and ease and freedom to the wearer.

'Next cut your leg seam very straight, and not hollow as is the common practice, and let your side seams be likewise straight from the knee up to within four inches of the hip: and observe you put in a gusset piece from that place on the outside of the hip, two inches and a half wide at the top, and cut taper or bevelled down to a point five inches long both of the outside and inside. When this done and your breeches are put on, you will find the ribs go straight down the thighs, which will avoid and provide against an abominable error in the trade, of twisting the ribs across the thighs, making them appear crooked, inwardly inclining, which seems to the spectator (according to the old vulgar adage) as if people were ill shap'd or knap knee'd. When you have got so far, cut your seat at the joining of the waistband, less by two inches double; and in making, let your knee-band be cut one inch longer than your measure, and back it on lining, and set it in with the knee-band to the breeches; this will keep them to the full size at the bottom, and make them lie agreeably, and rise to the springing of the calf of the leg if required. Let both the knee-band and the waist-band be beared on according to your length of them (both) and not the breeches, which though diametrically opposite to the common practice in use, we do affirm is positively right, and the true justified by and proved by long experience, and which will convince every practitioner on his first essay, if he does but adhere to the rule.' (Pages 97, 98.)

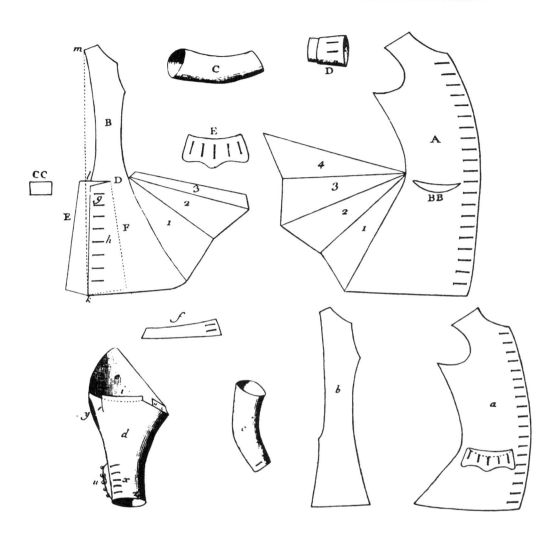

5. *Description des Arts et Métiers, L'Art du Tailleur*, M. de Garsault, Paris, 1769. The several parts that make a man's suit of clothes.

Fig. II.

Fig. III.

Fig. I.

6. *L'Art du Tailleur*
    Fig. I   Cloak with collar.
    Fig. II   Robe de chambre with separate sleeves.
    Fig. III Robe de chambre with sleeves 'en chemise', that is cut in with the
          body.
    H, gusset; E, belt; F, piece to lengthen sleeve.

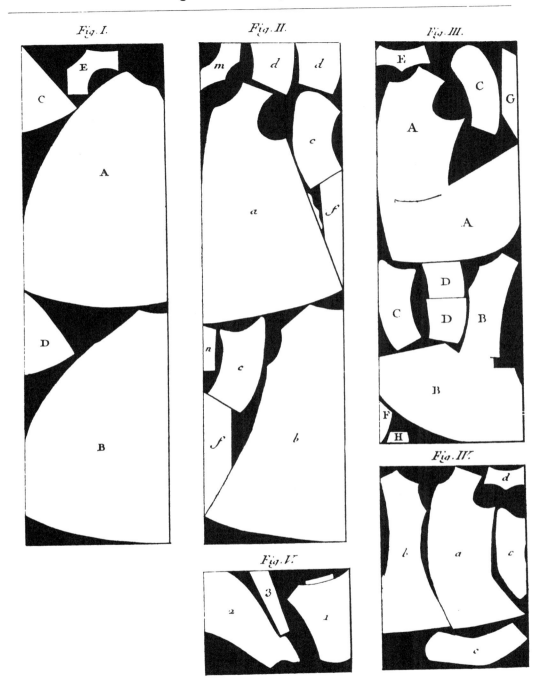

7. *L'Art du Tailleur*

Fig. I   Roquelaure cape.
Fig. II   Great-coat.
Fig. III Coat.

Fig. IV Waistcoat.
Fig. V Breeches.

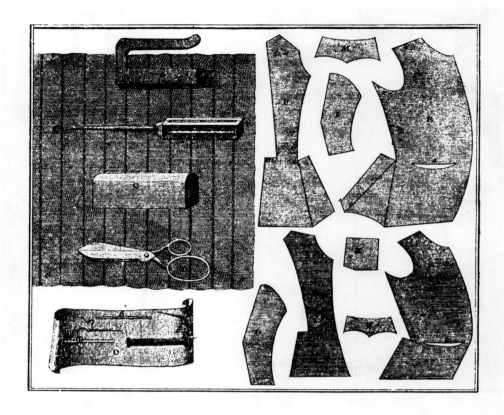

8. *Encyclopédie*, Panckóucke, *c.* 1780.
   Parts of a coat and waistcoat.
   A, iron; B, button-hole block; C, seam block; D, scissors; E, ironing cloth.

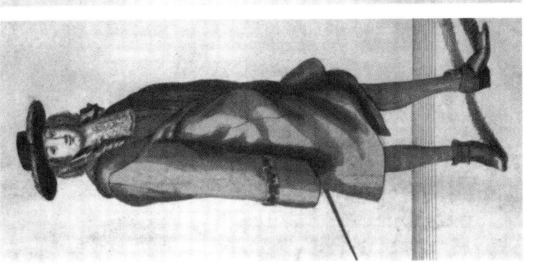

PLATE 8

(*left*) *c.* 1678. French Engraving. Great-coat. (*centre*) *c.* 1678. French Engraving. The coat at first was rather a dull garment and still retained the earlier ribbon accessories. (*right*) *c.* 1685. French Engraving. The coat skirts widen and the waistcoat sleeves sometimes appear below the shorter coat sleeves. Wigs general—dressed high and set in formal tight curls

PLATE 9

1729. (*above*) Day coats. Bag-wig, worn with a black ribbon round the neck—the 'Solitaire'. (*below*) Great-coats. The plaited queue was usual for travelling or military campaigns

Hérisset. 'Recueil des Differentes Modes du Temps'

PLATE 10

1745. *Joseph Highmore.* One of the illustrations to '*Pamela*'. The older man has the early wig and cravat, the younger one the full-skirted coat with the seams outlined with braid

PLATE 11

c. 1740. (See Diagram XX.) Full-skirted coat, made in the small-patterned figured silk which was very fashionable at this period. (The sleeves have been altered)

Gallery of Costume, Manchester

PLATE 12

c. 1760. A suit in cut velvet with fur and floral decoration which
was woven in position before the material was cut

Victoria and Albert Museum

PLATE 13

1777. *Moreau le Jeune.* '*La Grande Toilette*'. The central figure is in a full-dress embroidered suit. Accessories—a bouquet and fobs

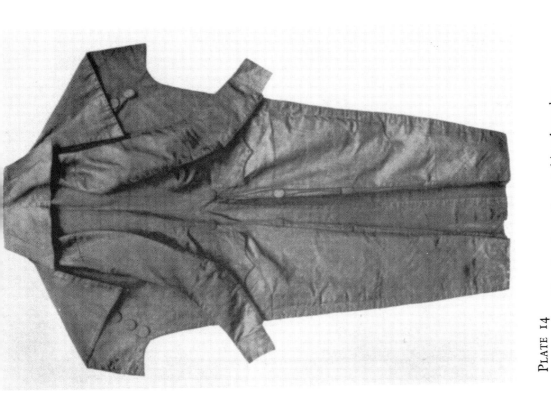

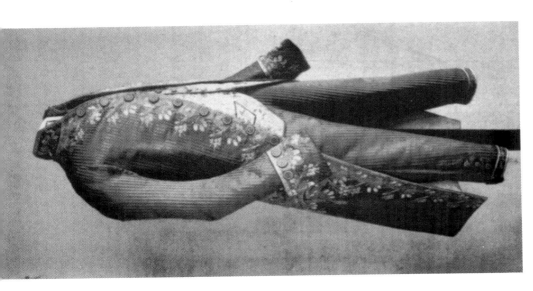

PLATE 14

(*left*) *c.* 1775. (See Diagram XXIII.) Full-dress embroidered suit, with matching breeches

(*right*) *c.* 1790. Brown silk coat. The cut is very similar to Diagram XXIX

Victoria and Albert Museum

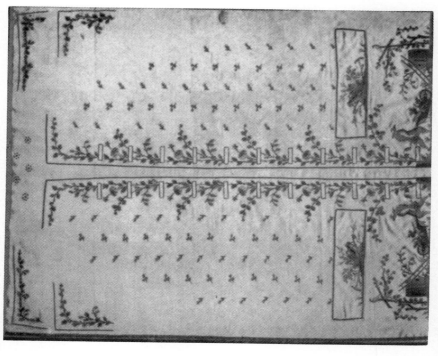

PLATE 15

(left) c. 1720. White satin waistcoat, heavily embroidered in gold and coloured silks. Similar to Diagram XXV
(right) c. 1780. Unmade waistcoat. Waistcoats embroidered with pictorial subjects were fashionable in the 80's

Victoria and Albert Museum

PLATE 16

c. 1770. Informal dress. A frock worn with a sporting type of waistcoat. Accessories—a
bicorne and Cadogan wig

PLATE 17

Late 1790's. *Carle Vernet*. 'Les Incroyables.' 'It is almost impossible to describe the 'Incroyables', with their square-cut coats and their hounds' ears locks of hair'

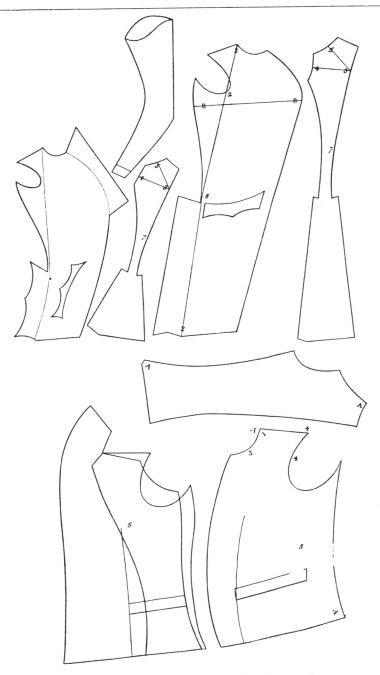

9. *The Taylor's Complete Guide*, London, 1796.
Coats and waistcoats.

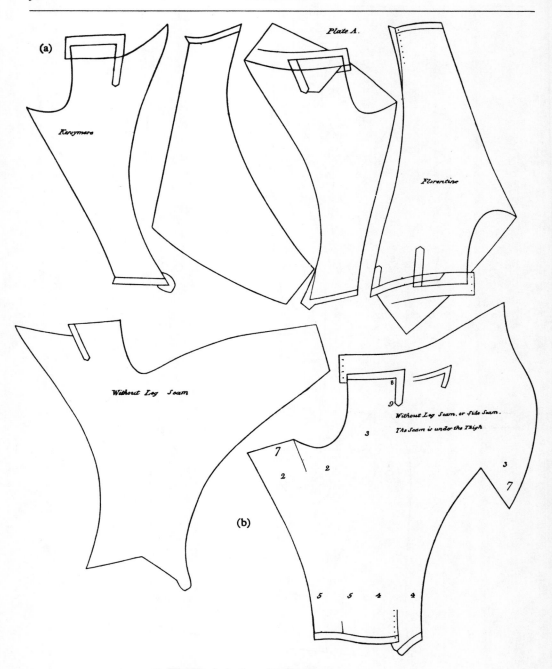

10. *The Taylor's Complete Guide.*
Breeches—(a) Two-seam leg. (b) One-seam leg.

Quotations from Contemporary Sources

Advertisements: A watch was found by a Gentleman 'that goes in a sad-coloured cloth suit, with a green shoulder-knot, figured with silver, and the facings of his coat of green velvet; he wears a light-coloured perriwig, with a grey hat, and a green taffety riband round it, and a sword knot of the same'.

A fellow who robbed Lord Windsor in April, 1682, had on 'a sad-coloured cloth suit, lined with a striped crape, with silver buttons and loops; a white hat, with gold twisted hat-band, and a dark-coloured camblet coat, lined with blue, the sleeves turned up with blue plush, with silver buttons and loops'.

J. P. MALCOLM, *Anecdotes of the Manners and Customs of London*

BILLS FROM THE ISHAM COLLECTION

For a Dove Couller Silke Coat and Breeches Brocaded with gold flowers the breeches with Large Cannons; and A white Satten wastcoat made, the Cannons and wastcoat Richly Laced with gold and Silluer Lace.   July the 2nd 1681

For Inward Linings to the Breeches	00 : 04 : 00
For Shamoy pocketts	00 : 02 : 06
For Callicoe Stayes to the Coate	00 : 04 : 00
For Sizeinge the Silke	00 : 05 : 00
For 9 doz and ½ of gold and Silke Coat buttons . . .	00 : 18 : 00
For 4 dozen and ½ of gold and Silluer brest to the wastcote and breeches	00 : 06 : 09
For Staying and Buckrum	00 : 02 : 00
For galloome	00 : 01 : 02
For Silke	00 : 06 : 00
For pocketts to the Coate	00 : 01 : 00
For persian Silke to Make under Cannons . . .	00 : 02 : 06

For tafaty Ribbon to bind them .   .   .   .   00 : 02 : 06
For a payre of Silke Stockins   .   .   .   .   00 : 14 : 00
For Making the Coat and Breeches and wastcoat Richly Laced and
    trimmed   .   .   .   .   01 : 04 : 00
                                                                    —————————
                                                                    04 : 13 : 00

For a Mixt grey Cloth Coate and Roule up breeches made buttond downe the sides
(October 5th 1679).

For A Blewish Silke Stuffe Coate and breeches to Buckle att knee with A garter and
knotts of Ribbon (August 7th 1681).

1692

Marriage of M. de Chartres and Mdlle. de Blois

Monsieur was in black velvet embroidered all over in gold and trimmed with rubies.
The king had a coat of gold brocade embroidered with silver, and a strap of very large
diamonds as a shoulder-knot, instead of the ribbon loops usually worn there. Monseigneur was in plain black velvet which enhanced the brilliance of the large diamonds
which decorated it; they belonged to the Crown and were worth several millions.

1697

Celebrations for the Marriage of Monseigneur le Duc de Bourgogne
and Mme. la Princesse de Savoie

On Wednesday, in the gallery at Versailles, there was the most magnificent ball that
had ever been given at Court. Words fail to describe the richness and diversity of the
clothes, they were so unimaginably brilliant that they dazzled the eyes. Monseigneur
was in cloth of gold, decorated with silver. The duc de Bourgogne was in black velvet,
and the duc d'Anjou and the duc du Berry in coloured velvets, all three embroidered
all over in gold and diamonds. Monsieur had the same suit as on the day of the wedding,
it was superb, of black velvet with very wide gold embroidered froggings set close
together, and large diamond buttons; his waistcoat was of gold and the rest of his
apparel of the same splendour. M. de Chartres was very rich and elegant in cloth of
gold trimmed with gold. Some of the courtiers had velvet suits, either embroidered or
with ornamental froggings, others were in gold brocade. There were a few plain coats
but most of them were embroidered, or had gold or silver lace. They all had very ornate
shoulder-knots, the sleeves covered with gold and silver lace and ribbons, gloves also
trimmed with ribbons, silk stockings of different colours with gold clocks, and ribbons
in their shoes.

1700

An edict is being prepared, which will soon appear, to curtail the excessive magnifi-
cence of gold and silver cloth.

                                                            DANGEAU, *Journal*

EARLY EIGHTEENTH-CENTURY ADVERTISEMENTS

Stolen—a new Cinnamon Colour Cloth Coat, Wastcoat, Breeches, Embroider'd with Silver 4 or 5 inches deep down before, and on the sleeves, and round the Pocket Holes and the Pockets and Knees of the Breeches. They are lin'd with a Sky Blue Silk.

Left in a Hackney Coach—a light brown colour'd Hanging Coat, with Long Sleeves, upper Cape Black Velvet, with Gold Buttons and Button Holes.

Taken from a Gentleman's House—a Dove Colour'd Cloth Suit embroider'd with Silver, and a pair of Silk Stockings of the same Colour; a Grey Cloth Suit with Gold Buttons and Holes; a Silk Drugget Salmon Colour'd Suit lin'd with white silk; a Silver Brocade Waistcoat trim'd with a knotted Silver Fringe, and lin'd with white Silk. A flour'd Saten Night gown, lin'd with a Pink colour'd Lustring, and a Cap and Slippers of the Same. A yellow Damask Nightgown lin'd with Blue Persian; a Scarlet net Sash to tie a Nightgown.

JOHN ASHTON, *Social Life in the Reign of Queen Anne*

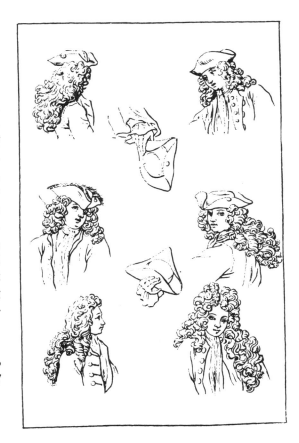

1702

Portrait of a Beau

He made a most magnificent figure. His periwig was large enough to have loaded a camel, and he had bestowed upon it at least a bushel of powder, I warrant you. His swordknot dangled upon the ground, and his steenkirk that was most agreeably discoloured with snuff from top to bottom, reached down to his waist. He carried his hat under his left arm, walked with hands in the waistband of his breeches, and his cane, that hung negligently down on a string from his right arm, trailed most harmoniously against the pebbles.

TOM BROWN,
Letters from the Dead to the Living

1711

August 16. The Skirt of your fashionable Coats forms as large a Circumference as our Petticoats; as these are set out with Whalebone, so are those with Wire, to encrease and sustain the Bunch of Fold that hangs down on each side, and the Hat, I perceive is decreased in just Proportion to our Head-dresses.

1714

September 4. Mr. Shapely is the prettiest Gentleman about Town. He is very tall, but not too tall neither . . . if you did but see how he rolls his Stocking! He has a thousand pretty Fancies.

The Spectator

EARLY EIGHTEENTH CENTURY

> *Each son of Sol, to make him look more big,*
> *Had on a large, grave, decent, three-tail'd wig;*
> *His clothes full-trimm'd, with button-holes behind;*
> *Stiff were the skirts, with buckram stoutly lined,*
> *The cloth, cut velvet, or more reverend black,*
> *Full made, and powder'd, half-way down his back,*
> *Large decent cuffs, which near the ground did reach,*
> *With half-a-dozen buttons fix'd on each.*

DR. DORAN, *Habits and Men*

1719

BILLS FROM THE VERNEY PAPERS

The Rt. Honble. Ld. Vext. Fermanagh—
               Dr. to Kath. Barradall & Samll. Palmer

Jan. 20	L.	S.	D.
Making a Collrd. Clo. Suite . .		18.	6.
Buttons for the Coat . . .		5.	0.
Small ditto		2.	9.
Dimity to Lyne the Body of Vest .		3.	0.
Double Wadding in Skirts . .		3.	0.
Shamoy Linings & Pocketts . .		5.	6.
Ribbon att Knee & Silk Puffs . .		2.	0.
Buckrum Canvas & Stays . .		3.	0.
Silk Thread and Twist . . .		5.	6.
	2.	8.	3.

French Satirical Song

The men, to emulate the ladies' present mode
Have brought the mocked-at pannier to their aid,
And for new finery extend their coats
With monstrous pleats ridiculously displayed.

FIRST HALF OF THE EIGHTEENTH CENTURY

I daresay it would interest you to hear of the style and the way Englishmen usually dress. They do not trouble themselves about dress, but leave that to their womenfolk. When the people see a well-dressed person in the streets, especially if he is wearing a braided coat, a plume in his hat, or his hair tied in a bow, he will, without a doubt, be called a 'French dog' twenty times perhaps before he reaches his destination. . . . Englishmen are usually very plainly dressed, they scarcely ever wear gold on their clothes; they wear little coats called 'frocks', without facings and without pleats, with a short cape above. Almost all wear small round wigs, plain hats, and carry canes in their hands, but no swords. Their cloth and linen are of the best and finest. You will see rich merchants and gentlemen thus dressed, and sometimes even noblemen of high rank, especially in the morning, walking through the filthy and muddy streets. The lower classes are usually well dressed, wearing good cloth and linen. Englishmen, however, are very lavish in other ways. They have splendid equipages and costly apparel when required. Peers and other persons of rank are richly dressed when they go to Court, especially on gala days, when their grand coaches, with their magnificent accoutrements, are used. . . .

The Quakers' mode of dressing is as curious as is their language; the men wear large, unlooped, flapping hats, without buttons or loops; their coats are as plain as possible, with no pleatings or trimmings, and no buttons or button-holes on the sleeves, pockets, or waists. If any brother were to wear ruffles to his shirts or powder on his hair, he would be considered impious. The most austere and zealous do not even wear shoe-buckles, but tie their shoes with cords. . . . Quakers' clothes, though of the simplest and plainest cut, are of excellent quality; their hats, clothes, and linen are of the finest.

CÉSAR DE SAUSSURE,
A Foreign View of England in the Reigns of George I and George II

M. de Gèvres said he was just leaving and put on his riding-coat (*redingote*)—this type of coat is of English origin, and very much worn at present when it is cold, or wet, and especially for riding.

E. J. F. BARBIER, *Journal*

1739

The Prince's Birthday

Nothing extraordinary among the men; much finery, chiefly brown, with gold or silver embroidery, and rich waistcoats. My Lord Baltimore was in light brown and silver, his coat lined quite throughout with ermine.

MRS. DELANY, *Autobiography*

1742

I have been told he had on a cut velvet coat of cinnamon colour, lined with a pink satten, embroidered all over with gold; his waistcoat, which was cloth of silver, was embroidered with gold likewise. I cannot be particular as to the rest of his dress; but it was all in the French fashion, for Bellarmine (that was his name) was just arrived from Paris. . . . 'Yes, madam; this coat, I assure you, was made at Paris, and I defy the best English taylor even to imitate it. There is not one of them can cut, madam; they can't cut. If you observe how this coat is turned, and this sleeve: a clumsy English rascal can do nothing like it. Pray, how do you like my liveries? . . . All French, I assure you, except for the greatcoats; I never trust anything more than a greatcoat to an Englishman.'

HENRY FIELDING, *The Adventures of Joseph Andrews*

1745

Court Ball to Celebrate the Dauphin's Marriage

All the men who are going to danse must wear their hair long, with long curls, and those who are not dancing, are allowed two little cadenettes (small plaits), but not a bag, although this is the present style worn by all courtiers; evidently that is not considered suitable for a ceremonial occasion. . . . M. le marquis de Mirepois has hired three suits for 6,000 livres, each of which he will wear one day only and then return them to the tailor.

E. J. F. BARBIER, *Journal*

1750

London—The men go out early in the morning, dressed in frocks, either to take a walk or a ride; at their return they generally dine at a tavern; they most of them go incognito to the Play or to Vauxhall; it is not thought necessary to dress except to appear at the Opera or at the places where they are invited to dine.

MME. DE BOCAGE, *Letters concerning England, Holland and Italy*

1752

Paris—Our next Care was to equip ourselves in the Fashion of the Country. Accordingly we sent for a Taylor, and Jack Commons, who jabbers a little French, directed him to make us two Suits; which he brought us the next Morning at Ten o'Clock, and made complete Frenchmen of us. But for my part, Harry, I was so damned uneasy in a full-dressed Coat, with hellish long Skirts, which I had never been used to, that I thought myself as much deprived of my Liberty, as if I had been in the Bastile; and I frequently sighed for my little loose Frock, which I look upon as an Emblem of our happy Constitution; for it lays a Man under no uneasy Restraint, but leaves it in his Power to do as he pleases.

Gray's-Inn Journal

1766

I ride in a chair with my hands in a muff,
And have bought a silk coat and embroider'd the cuff;
But the weather was cold, and the coat it was thin,
So the taylor advis'd me to line it with skin:
But what with my Nivernois hat can compare?
Bag-wig, and lac'd ruffles, and black solitaire?
And what can a man of true fashion denote,
Like an ell of good ribbon ty'd under the throat?
My buckles and box are in exquisite taste;
The one is of paper, the other of paste.

Anstey, *The New Bath Guide*

177–

It will scarcely be credited now, that the fops and macaronies of this date actually wore their hair frizzled out on each side the head to more than the breadth of the visage, and that a solid pound of hair powder was wasted in dressing a fool's head.

Ranelagh—It was the custom for gentlemen to buy, in the ante-room, nosegays, myrtles, hyacinthes, roses, etc., etc., not only to wear themselves, but also to present some of them to ladies. There were no cropped heads, trousers, or shoe-strings seen here—such dresses would not have been admitted. Ranelagh was the *élite* of fashion. The gentlemen wore powder, frills, ruffles, and had gold headed canes, etc., etc., forming a great contrast to the dandyism of the present day. . . .

As for the men, speaking comparatively of the present costume, the greater part of them had the appearance of gentlemen. On their heads which were powdered, they had high toupées, queues, grand *cadogans*, swords by their sides, projecting frills, stocks, ruffles, cocked hats, and buckles, some with their chapeau-bras and bag.

Henry Angelo, *Reminiscences*

1770

Bills from the Gallery of English Costume, Manchester

Nov. 20th Mr. Grant to Robert Johnson dr.

	£	s	d
A fine Blue Cloth frock & breeches, lin'd with Ratinett & gilt Buttons	4.	16.	6.
6 yds. Gold plaited lace @ 15/	4.	10.	0.
Gold Vellum & thread to work the holes & 20 Gold spangled buttons		17.	6.
Linnen & Materials		10.	6.

1771

	£	s	d
Feb. 5 To a pair fine worsted knit breeches	1.	1.	0.

1775

March 6 Captain Hackman Dr. to Charles Pearce & Son

	£	s	d
Making a Pearl Colld Cloth Coat and Breech. Edges Bound with Silk Braid and a Pea Green florentine Silk Wastct. Laced with 2 Stripes Silver Lace	1.	5.	0.
2¾ yards surfine Cloth @ 18/	2.	9.	6.
2 yards Rich florentine Silk @ 14/	1.	8.	0.
5 yards Rich Silk Serge to face, etc. @ 6/	1.	10.	0.
Holland sleeves and Pocketts		3.	6.
Callico Body lining		4.	6.
Fine Holland to interline do.		2.	6.
Shallon for back		2.	6.
Dimothy Wastd. and Pocketts		3.	0.
1½ Doz. fine Wire Coat buttons @ 2/6		3.	9.
2 Doz Breast do @ 1/3		2.	6.
½ Doz Rich Silver Striped do		10.	6.
Silk Garters		2.	0.
Paid for Rich Silk Band and Tassells		18.	0.
5½ yards Rich Silver Striped Lace @ 4/6	1.	4.	9.
Sewing Silk and Twist		5.	0.
Buckram Canvas and Stays		4.	6.
Making a Pr. Sea Green florentine silk Breeches . . .		5.	0.
2½ yards Rich florentine Silk @ 14/	1.	15.	0.
Brown Holland Interlinings and Pocketts . . .		4.	6.
Buttons and facings		1.	6.
Sewing Silk and twist		1.	6.
Buckram Canvas and Stays		1.	0.

Making a Striped Cotton Dble Breasted Wastt. faced the same and all materials . . . . 18. 0.

July 11. A Green florentine Silk Wastt. Laced with Stripped Lace Altered and made fashionable and Shorter . . . . . 5. 0.

1772

Macaronis—They make a most ridiculous figure with hats of an inch in the brim, that do not cover but lie upon the head, with about two pounds of ficticious hair, formed into what is called a club, hanging down their shoulders as white as a baker's sack. The end of the skirt of their coat reaches the first button of their breeches which are either brown-striped or white, as wide as a Dutchman's; their coat sleeves are so tight they can with much difficulty get their arms through their cuffs which are about an inch deep; & their shirt sleeve without pleats, is pulled over a bit of Trolly lace. Their legs are at times covered with all the colours of the rainbow; even flesh-coloured & green silk stockings are not excluded. Their shoes are scarce slippers, & their buckles are within an inch of the toe. Such a figure, essenced & perfumed, with a bunch of lace sticking out under its chin, puzzles the common passenger to determine the thing's sex.

Town and Country Magazine

178–

In the morning the king (Louis XVI) wore a grey coat until it was time for his toilette. Then he put on a cloth suit, often brown, with a steel or silver sword. But on Sundays and ceremonial occasions his suits were of very beautiful materials, embroidered in silks and pailettes. Often, as the fashion then was, the velvet coat was entirely covered with little spangles which made it very dazzling. The diamonds belonging to the Crown added their brilliance, the 'Regent' was his hat button; and the 'Sancy' was on the epaulet which held the blue ribbon (St. Esprit), worn on ceremonial occasions.

FELIX HÉZECQUES, *Souvenirs d'un Page de la Cour de Louis XVI*

1778 August

Prologue to the new Comedy of *The Suicide*

> *'Tis now the reigning taste with belle and beau*
> *Their art and skill in coachmanship to show:*
> *Nobles contend who throws a whip the best,*
> *From head to foot like hackney-coachmen dress'd.*

1782 September

Dear Madam we wish to remonstrate with these smart gentlemen, and tell them, they are incapable of correcting the foibles in the ladies' dresses, till they have established a criterion for their own . . . can they point out of what use are the high-crowned hats, their shoes tied with strings, the number of buttons lately added to their coats: of what real service that ponderosity at their watches and canes?

1787 August

Epilogue to *She Stoops to Conquer*

> *Look round this town and view with wond'ring eyes,*
> *In quick succession, how the fashions rise;*
> *The Beau, who once in gay brocade could trip,*
> *Wears his round hat, his boots, and smacks his whip.*

Ladies' Magazine

1786

One thing is certain just now, and that is that the inclination not only for the fashions, but also for the customs and habits of this rival nation (England) has never been carried so far in France.

GRIMM, *Correspondence*

c. 1788

Young men are mad about horses, and for some time have ignored the ladies of the Opera—the courtisanes resent this treatment; the young men take them out less and their horses more: until the evening all dress like grooms; they look awkward in dress clothes. . . .

The men wear square-tailed coats with very long waists: the skirts reach the knees; the breeches reach the calves: the shoes are pointed and as thin as paper: the head rests on a cravat as if on a cushion shaped like a wash-basin: or with others the cravat envelops the chin. Hair is frissed or parted on the forehead; long strands flutter behind the ears: it is plaited behind. No more cuffs, no more jabots: very fine linen. A gold pin shaped like a star or a butterfly, shows off the whiteness of the shirt. An individual so dressed walks like Hercules, a stick in his hand, and spectacles to his nose.

LOUIS-SÉBASTIEN MERCIER, *Tableau de Paris*

1788

The Queen's Birthday

His Majesty appeared in the evening in a suit of brown velvet richly embroidered. . . . The Prince of Wales was arrayed in a superb dress: the coat was a pale ruby ground, covered with a rich work of white and silver, and beautifully embroidered down the seams with silver; the star of St. George was formed of brilliantes; the loop also was of diamonds; the waistcoat was of white and silver, highly rich and beautiful. The hat in which his highness appeared in the evening at the ball, had a beautiful brilliancy.

The Ladies' Magazine

1790

BILL FROM THE GALLERY OF ENGLISH COSTUME, MANCHESTER

July 3rd. Captn. Willm Mansel to Peter Donelly

	£	s	d
a blue lapelld coat faced with buff kerseymere with 4 Dozen of Solid gilt Buttons	3.	6.	0.
a Collar of uncut velvet to Do.		7.	0.
a fine Green Coat faced with Do & Scarlet Collar	3.	8.	0.
a Mixture Frock Lapelld	2.	18.	0.
a Collar of uncut Velvet to Do.		7.	0.
a double brested great Coat of Mixture Cloth	3.	13.	6.
To 2 pr of buff Kerseymere Breeches with Silk strings to the Knee & 2 Buff Kerseymere Waistcoats	4.	10.	0.
To 4 prs of Nankeen Breeches . . . 15/	3.	0.	0.
To 4 India Dimity Waistcoats . . . 15/	3.	0.	0.

1791

There is to be a ball at Windsor on Friday for the Prince's birthday, which has not lately been noticed there. Lord Lorn and seven other young men of fashion were invited to it. It seems they now crop their hair short and wear no powder, which not being the etiquette yet, the youths, instead of representing that they are not fit to appear so docked, sent excuses that they were going out of town, or were unavoidably engaged.

HORACE WALPOLE, *Letters*

END OF THE EIGHTEENTH CENTURY

It is almost impossible to describe the 'Incroyables', with their square-cut coats and their hounds' ears locks of hair. Just imagine—they wore medallions, lorgnettes, chains, ear-rings with cameos, and had their cadenettes caught up with a comb. They had the most ridiculous stockings you have ever seen, for they were striped across so as to make large coloured rings round their legs. They also surrounded their necks with an extraordinary style of cravat.

LA MARQUISE DE CRÉQUY, *Souvenirs*

1794

For these last three or four years, if a man has been to Court he cannot go, without some singularity, to dine out or to an assembly without putting on a frock. . . . I have also heard Fox say that the neglect of dress in people of fashion had he thought contributed much to remove the barriers between them and the vulgar and to propagate levelling and equalising notions.

So late as the years 1788 and 1789, at some great assembly given during the Regency business by the Duchess of Portland, all the men went full-dressed.

LORD GLENBERVIE, *Journals*

1794

In 1777 society was subjected, indeed, to fetters from which we have since emancipated ourselves—those of dress, etiquette, and form. The lapse of two centuries could scarcely have produced a greater alteration in these particulars than have been made by about forty years. That costume which is now (1815) confined to the levée or the drawing-room was then worn by persons of condition with few exceptions, every where and every day. Mr. Fox and his friends, who might be said to dictate to the town, affecting a style of neglect about their persons, and manifesting a contempt of all the usages hitherto established, first threw a sort of discredit on dress. From the House of Commons and the clubs in St. James's Street the contagion spread through the private assemblies of London. But though gradually undermined and insensibly perishing of an atrophy, dress never totally fell till the era of Jacobinism and of equality in 1793 and 1794. It was then that pantaloons, cropped hair, and shoe-strings, as well as the total abolition of buckles and ruffles, together with the disuse of hair-powder, characterised the men.

SIR NATHANIEL WILLIAM WRAXALL, *Historical and Posthumous Memoirs*

Part Three

1800-1900

1800-1900

Whereas the eighteenth century was characterized by its attention to cut, the nineteenth was notable for its concentration on fit. There were a few innovations but no drastic changes as far as cut and design were concerned. This state of affairs was due to several causes, the main one being the adoption of cloth and a more scientific approach to the whole technique of tailoring. Social conditions directed what might have been a passing phase into an entirely new attitude towards men's clothes and their production.

The fashionable coat of the 1770's hung loose from the chest, for it was not possible to fit the coat close to the body with only two side seams placed so far back. Consequently the fit of this particular suit had to be in the waistcoat and breeches. If, however, the coat was cut in cloth, a much more pliable material than tightly woven silk, shrinking and stretching by the tailor's iron could mould it and give a more subtle fit, even if the coat was worn buttoned.

By the end of the eighteenth century English tailors became the leaders of men's fashions, because their long experience and appreciation of the subtleties of cloth had developed their skill and they gave style and elegance to the practical country coats and so made them acceptable for fashionable wear. Beau Brummell, not an innovator but a perfectionist, set the seal on this new fashion by removing the odour of the stables. He had the floppy cravat starched, the muddy boots polished, and above all, he demanded perfect cut and fit.

The end of the eighteenth and the beginning of the nineteenth century was another transition period. Court and country styles intermingled and produced a diversity of coats, long and short, with all manner of collars, capes, revers, tags, froggings, etc. Early in the new century these styles became stabilized, and during the rest of the century the changes were in comparative trifles.

DRESS-COAT

By the nineteenth century the cut-in tail coat was adopted for all dress occasions, both day and evening, except Court. It became the 'dress-coat'. It was cut away horizontally just above the normal waist line, and the front tails were stitched to the back panel with a small pleat. The body had three seams only—centre back, and two side seams set close to the centre back one. For day wear it was single or double-breasted, for evening, by the 1820's, 'it should, if any thing, be even too small to meet across the waist and chest, so that it may sit open and display the waistcoat, shirt and cravat to the most advantage'. About 1818 fashion demanded a longer body and a tighter fit in the waist, so the crease, inevitable at the waist-line in front, was eliminated by making a dart, called a 'fish', and by the early 1820's the dart became a seam and the body and front tails were cut as separate pieces. When the waist descended again darts became necessary for fit at the sides below the armhole, and by 1840 they too were seams. The body of the coat had now five seams and was made from six separate pieces. This method of cutting the body was also applied to all nineteenth-century coats which had fitted bodies and separate skirts or tails. During the 1820's and 30's the collar was large and very stiff, like a horse collar, the fronts padded and the sleeves at the same time gathered on top. By the 1850's the fashion line was long-bodied and sleek. By 1860 the dress-coat was no longer worn during the day, but it continued to be, and still is, worn as formal evening dress. The basic principle of cutting a dress-coat has not changed since 1840, but throughout its long life it has undergone many slight variations of proportion—length of tails, shape and size of collar, revers, waist high or low, etc.

Morning or Riding Coat

The riding coat was another tail coat, but with sloping front edges instead of the horizontal front cut. As riding was a popular morning exercise for a gentleman this coat came to be known as a 'morning coat', and was also worn on more informal occasions. During the second half of the century it grew in favour and from 1880 was worn on formal occasions, eventually taking the place of the frock-coat. It is still formal day wear today. The body of this coat was cut like that of the dress-coat and followed the same changes.

Frock-coat

The frock-coat appeared about 1816. It was probably of military origin as on its first appearance it was worn buttoned to the neck, with a standing collar. It derived from the great-coat but the body was always fitted—first dart then seam at waist, and the skirts—very full—hung straight down from the waist centre front. In its early days this coat went through several experimental phases. The body might still look military, with braid froggings and standing collar, or have revers and turned down collar, the skirts short or long. Finally the body was the same as that of the dress-coat (single- or double-breasted) and the skirt about knee length. A slightly looser fitting variation with long skirts became a 'top-frock coat'. The frock-coat was at first worn as undress, but by 1850 it came into use for formal wear when it replaced the dress-coat. In the 1860's, in common with all the other clothes of that time, a looser fit and less material in the skirts gave it a much straighter line. It now became a very worthy and somewhat dull garment, a coat for the well-to-do and professional classes—the hall-mark of Victorian respectability. It is true that the frock-coat did smarten up again in the 1890's with a more fitted body and fuller, longer skirts, but by then the morning coat was taking over, and the frock-coat only just survived the Edwardian age.

GREAT-COAT, ETC.

During the first half of the nineteenth century great-coats were much in evidence and worn in town irrespective of weather conditions. The two main styles were, first, the great-coat, or surtout, which was a double-breasted coat with the fronts cut straight but the side seams and shoulder seams towards the back like the dress-coat. There was a pleat in the front skirt where it was stitched to the back and sometimes flap pockets were inserted at hip level into the side seams, the centre back skirt being open with a slight lap over. It was worn very long—down to the ankles—with a collar and sometimes a cape. The other style was the looser box coat whose side seams swung out from under the arms; it might have a belt or just the back fullness held in by a strap. It fastened with buttons or more usually with tabs. Its chief characteristic was still the layers of shoulder capes. Variations towards the middle of the century were the frock great-coat (with waist seam) and the paletot, a kind of short great-coat.

The second half of the century produced more practical styles for travelling or country wear: the 'Inverness cape' appeared in the 1850's and was a loose overcoat with arm length cape. In later versions the cape was not completed behind. The 'Ulster' was another long loose coat, but always worn with a belt and usually a detachable hood. There were also several styles of top coats for smarter wear, such as the 'Chesterfield' which was cut straight with no waist seam, and often no centre back seam and usually worn shorter than the other types of overcoats. A longer and smarter version of this coat appeared in the 1890's and as its name suggests—the 'Paddock', or the 'Ascot' was designed for the sporting fraternity.

Capes were worn in the evening by the smart man, and rougher types of capes were practical country wear.

PILOT COAT, OR PALETOT

The pilot coat, or paletot, was the original of all the loosely cut garments which appeared from the 1830's onwards and which inspired the more casual coats and sports wear of the end of the century. *The Tailor's Guide*, Compaing and Devere, 1855, gives a good description of them: 'We term Paletot, or any other name you may prefer, a garment having no seam across the waist, and in which the skirt is of one piece with the forefront. There extends a great variety of style in this garment, resulting from the place of the seams, which may be combined in a hundred different ways, as also from extra looseness given either behind, in front, in the sides, or all round. Paletots may be cut tight-fitting in the body, in order to be worn without an undergarment, but this case is so very rare that we may nearly say it does not exist. Even in summer, paletots are worn as overgarments in the night or in case of bad weather, or, if worn alone, they are intended to leave the wearer easy in his motions. In general, a paletot is a garment intended to be worn alone or over another garment, at pleasure. Paletots are the starting point of all fancy garments.' Indeed, about the middle of the century there was a great variety of fancy garments.

LOUNGE JACKET

From all the offshoots the most important one to survive was the 'lounge jacket'. This was derived from the simple two-seamed paletot by taking a long dart from the under-arm slightly forward and extending it down to the waist, thereby giving it more fit. By 1870 the lounge jacket, worn with matching waistcoat and trousers, had become very popular for informal wear. In 1888 appeared the 'dress lounge' for informal evening wear, known from 1896 as the 'dinner jacket'. When the frock-coat was discarded and the morning coat became a coat for special occasions the lounge suit was accepted for smart day wear, and in the present day has assumed all the respectability of the Victorian frock coat. A variation 'suitable for any kind of outdoor exercise', was the 'Norfolk jacket' which appeared in the 1870's. It also was a two-seamed jacket but was cut full and the fullness arranged in box pleats, two in the front and two in the back. It had a belt and was worn with 'knickerbockers'—knee breeches with legs cut loose and gathered into a knee-band.

WAISTCOAT

Waistcoats were usually worn the fashionable waist length, single- or double-breasted, with or without collars and revers, usually straight across the waist, but from 1825 to the 1850's slightly pointed at the centre front. The standing collar was seen until 1830. In the 1830's and 40's the fronts were padded and a small dart into the armhole and another under the lapel helped to give the fashionable rounded-chest look. From 1820 to 1840 two or more waistcoats were often worn at the same time. Almost to the end of the century waistcoats were the most decorative article of men's nineteenth-century dress, being usually made in rich materials, plain or patterned, and often brightly coloured. In the early 1850's waistcoats began to match the trousers and by the late 60's there were three-piece matching suits. For formal wear, however, waistcoats were usually lighter in colour and material. For evening wear waistcoats were always white or black. Black was more informal but was correct formal wear from the 1860's to the end of the 80's.

BREECHES, PANTALOONS, TROUSERS

Breeches were the correct wear with the evening dress coat until *c.* 1810, and were also often worn in the day with tail coats until *c.* 1830, and always with Court dress. They continued to be worn by the unfashionable until well into the century, and for certain sports and also for country wear. The front of the breeches was cut with flaps, or 'falls', 5 inches to 8 inches wide.

Pantaloons were very generally worn until the middle of the nineteenth century and replaced breeches for formal wear. They fitted closely, like tights. Early versions were often cut with one seam only, down the outside leg, but by 1810 with two leg seams. Until 1817 the pantaloons were calf length, and then, they extended to the ankles with a side slit which buttoned. Straps under the instep kept them taut, but for evening wear the stockings had to be visible. Moschettos were a variation of pantaloons with gaiters attached. They did not survive the 1830's.

Trousers appeared very early in the century for informal day wear, and were accepted for informal evening wear from 1817. By 1825 they were in general use, though pantaloons were still considered correct evening wear until the middle of the century. At first trousers were cut so tight they were barely distinguishable from the pantaloons, and like them were only calf length but cut the same width at the bottom as at the calf. By 1817 they reached to the shoe, and were worn with straps until the middle of the century—sometimes with gaiter bottoms, 1820–55. Throughout the century they were cut narrow with slight variations. In the 1870's and 80's the legs were sometimes tight at the knees and expanded below. In the late 80's the bottom of the legs began to be turned up. From 1840 all trousers were cut with a centre front fly.

There were, however, two main types of wider-cut trousers. First the 'Cossacks' which were inspired by the Czar's visit to London in 1814. They were cut very full and gathered into the waistband and also round the ankles. By the 1820's they were more usually pleated into the waist and fitted the ankles, and were worn until the middle of the century. The second type, known as 'Peg-top' trousers, appeared *c.* 1857 and lasted about ten years. They were very similar to the later Cossack style.

MATERIALS, ETC.

During the first half of the nineteenth century a variety of coat styles, with flamboyant accessories and in a wide colour range, showed how untrimmed cloth could command its own distinctive style. It is true that the high stocks and cravats, the small waists and tightly fitting pantaloons must have occasioned a certain discomfort, but the Dandies and Exquisites who wore them were gentlemen of leisure who could restrain their actions to suit their clothes. There was, however, by the middle of the century a prosperous rising middle class who created a new demand for gentlemanly well-cut confortable clothes—businessmen who had no time for the foibles of fashion—and so the earlier dashing lines sobered up, tailors co-operated by concentrating on fit and execution, and by the end of the century men's clothes had become practical, dull and uniform. Superb materials and expert tailoring alone distinguished a gentleman of fashion from his fellows.

Throughout the first half of the century the coat, waistcoat, and leg garments were of different colours and materials. The coats were usually in dark shades of blue, green, claret, brown and black, but from 1860 onwards black predominated for formal wear. Lighter colours and lighter materials were worn in summer. Early in the century evening full dress coats might be in dark colours like the day coat, but soon dark blue and black only were acceptable—and from 1860, black only.

The fashionable coat materials were firm woollen cloths with a smooth dress surface, such as superfine, broadcloth, kerseymere, etc. During the first half of the century the pantaloons and trousers were almost always light in colour and the materials used usually lighter in weight than for the coat, these were jersey-weaves, merinos, doeskins, cassimirs, kerseymeres, etc.; for summer nankeen, a heavy twilled cotton, or drill, a stout twilled linen, were very popular. From the late 1840's tweeds and worsteds in stripes, checks and plaids began a new trend in materials though at first only used for trousers and casual jackets. For evening dress pantaloons or trousers were generally of kerseymere or cashmere in white or black until 1840, but after that date always black. The more casual styles of coats as worn from the second half of the century were made in tweeds, worsteds, etc., and by the last quarter of the century fine worsteds and vicunas were replacing superfine and woollen cloth for dress-coats. Great-coats were of thick woollen cloth such as box cloth, beaver, melton and cheviot, but the Inverness and the Ulster were usually of tweed. Flannel was first used for suits in the early 90's.

Velvet and silk facings to collars and revers are seen throughout the century. From the late 1830's braid was used to bind the edges, and piped, bound, or braided edges were very fashionable from the 1850's onwards. The outer side seam of the trousers was also often covered with braid. The facings, braiding, as well as the style of collars, revers, pockets, buttons, etc., were details which varied from year to year.

COLLARS, STOCKS, CRAVATS

Neckwear was a very important addition to men's dress in the nineteenth century especially during the first half when it was one of the principal vanities of the Dandies.

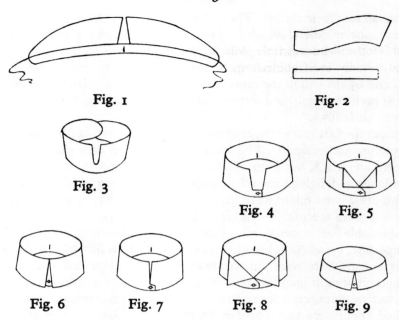

Fig. 1

Fig. 2

Fig. 3

Fig. 4

Fig. 5

Fig. 6   Fig. 7   Fig. 8   Fig. 9

COLLAR

At first the collar was attached to the shirt; it was worn turned up and deep enough to appear over the stock or cravat. A separate collar appeared in the 1820's (Figs. 1, 2). An unstarched collar worn turned down was very rare before 1850 and was always very informal wear. From the middle of the century the starched collar, either worn upright (Fig. 3) or double, began to diminish in height and was worn quite narrow until the 90's when it steadily rose again and by 1896 reached three inches. There were a variety of collar styles in the 1890's (Figs. 4–9).

STOCKS

A stock was a shaped band fastened at the back of the neck with ties, a buckle, or hook and eye. Stocks were made from horsehair or buckram, usually with a shaped centre front seam and the edges bound with leather; they were then covered with velvet, satin or silk, cut on the cross with no centre front seam (Fig. 1). Extravagant styles reached high on the cheeks and extended to the verge of the chin. Stocks had been part of military costume from the beginning of the eighteenth century but were only brought into fashion in 1822 by George IV—the full-dress stock was named after him:

    Fig. 2. 'Royal George'—Black velvet with a satin bow.

    Fig. 3. 'Plain Bow'—All black silk and straight-sided.

    Fig. 4. 'Military'—Black corded silk, no tie, mounted on leather beaten to shape on
        a block.

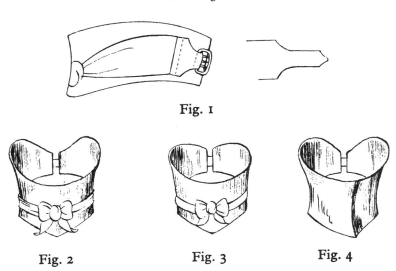

Fig. 1

Fig. 2   Fig. 3   Fig. 4

Stocks were less fashionable after *c.* 1840 but continued to be worn by older men though later versions were not nearly so extravagant in shape.

CRAVATS

The cravat was a large square, or triangle, of lawn, muslin, or silk, folded cornerwise into a band and usually starched by the laundress (Figs. 1, 2, p. 120). Black or coloured cravats were considered very undress, patterned white might be worn for half-dress but they always had to be plain white for balls and soirées. Sometimes the cravat was folded over a stiffener which was made from buckram or whalebone and bound with leather (Fig. 3). Considerable art and patience were required to arrange a cravat and many variations were devised:

Fig. 4. 'À l'Américaine'—Striped material, starched and worn with a stiffener.

Fig. 5. 'Collier de Cheval'—Black, striped or spotted, unstarched but worn with a stiffener.

Fig. 6. 'À la Byron'—Black or white, folded as in Fig. 1, not starched, worn in summer and for long journeys.

Fig. 7. 'En Cascade'—Unstarched, for valets or butlers.

Fig. 8. 'À la Bergami'—Folded as in Fig. 2 with the ends tied behind the back.

Fig. 9. 'De Bal'—White, slightly starched and folded as in Fig. 2, it is attached to the braces or tied behind the back.

Fig. 10. 'Mathématique'—Black taffeta folded over a stiffener.

Fig. 11. 'À la Gastronome'—No starch but worn with a stiffener; the knot is elastic and so can be loosened in cases of indigestion, apoplexy and fainting.

Cravats with or without stiffeners, were worn for sport and by the elderly until almost the end of the century, but by the 1850's the fashionable cravat had become a made-up

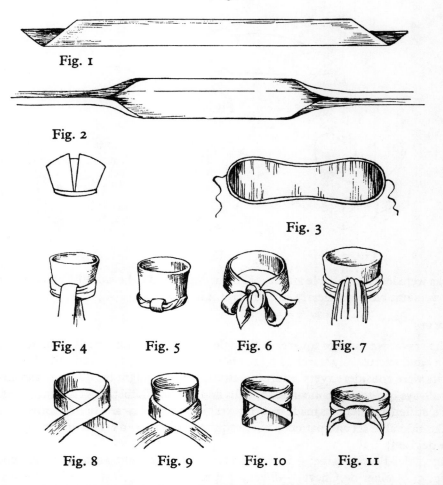

Fig. 1

Fig. 2

Fig. 3

Fig. 4   Fig. 5   Fig. 6   Fig. 7

Fig. 8   Fig. 9   Fig. 10   Fig. 11

band—the 'necktie'. This might be moderately broad and tied in a flat bow or folded and fastened with a pin, or there was a very much narrower version, the 'shoe-tie', which also tied in a bow or was knotted with long ends. From the early 60's to the end of the 80's coats were worn buttoned very high, and consequently very little neckwear was visible. The smarter 90's produced a variety of neckties and the old kerchief returned as a 'scarf'.

CONSTRUCTION OF NINETEENTH-CENTURY COATS

In the first half of the nineteenth century the woollen cloth used for the fashionable coats was so firmly woven and heavily milled that the edges could be cut and left raw. The foreparts and the collar were faced with the same cloth if a richer material, such as velvet, was not used. The centre fronts of the body, sometimes across the shoulders at the back, and the collar were interlined with canvas. The collar was stiffened and moulded to shape by sewing the canvas interlining (cut on the bias) to the collar of the coat with many small 'padding-stitches'—closer together for the rise and farther apart for the fall. Little padding was used except in the chest. The sleeves were commonly lined with white linen and the front skirts with a heavy cotton, or sometimes with a richer material of the same or contrasting colour as the coat. The back body and skirts were unlined. The skirt was always open centre back but the front skirt, with a slight pleat or fold, sewn to the back skirt.

During the second half of the nineteenth century there was a great advance in the technique of making and finishing men's clothes. By 1880 the edges were turned in except sometimes the bottom of the frock and tail coats (according to the material used). Overcoats, if cut from the heavily milled beavers or meltons, would still have all edges left raw—usually double-stitched. Coats were cut looser, especially round the armholes, and consequently there was an increase in interlining and paddings. The canvas in the forepart was darted to take the shape of the chest, wadding graded to shape was laid round the back and front of the armhole, the shoulder held out by inserting a three-cornered pad made from two or three layers of canvas, and a little padding was also placed in the sleeve head. Shoulder padding was known as 'American shoulders' and even in the late 1870's some men still preferred to have their coats made to fit the body closely without padding. From the last quarter of the century coats were completely lined—usually black Italian for the body but the skirts with the same material as used for the coat, or for very fashionable wear silk or satin. In the 1860's and 70's quilted linings were popular in town overcoats, but the Inverness and the Ulster were usually lined with brightly coloured plaids. Throughout the whole process of making a coat the tailor's iron was used with great skill and the cloth and canvas moulded by stretching and shrinking.

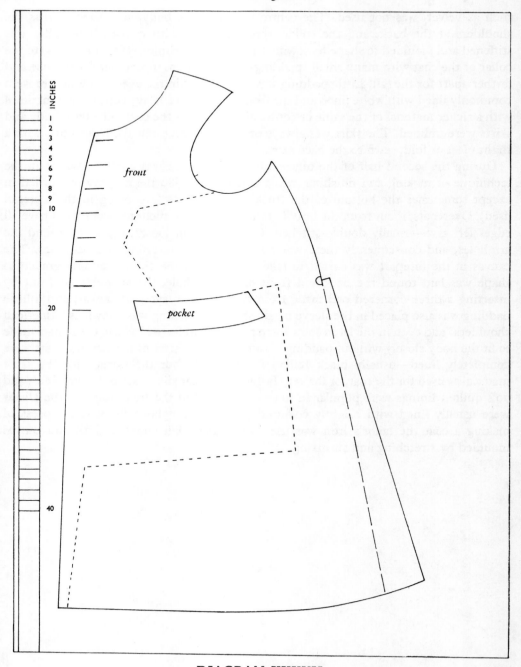

DIAGRAM XXXVII

GREAT-COAT *c.* 1810. Heavily-milled brown woollen cloth, unlined but the fronts and collar are faced with the same cloth (dotted lines). The side seams are stitched from the pockets downwards, the centre back skirt open. All edges cut. *Victoria and Albert Museum*

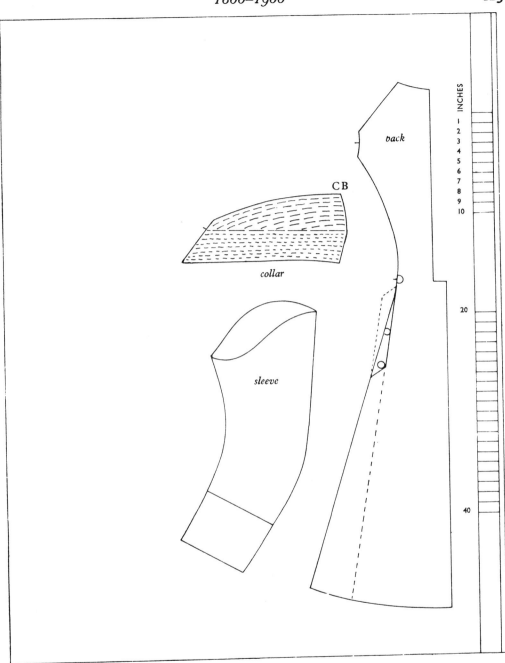

back

CB

collar

sleeve

INCHES

1
2
3
4
5
6
7
8
9
10

20

40

DIAGRAM XXXVII

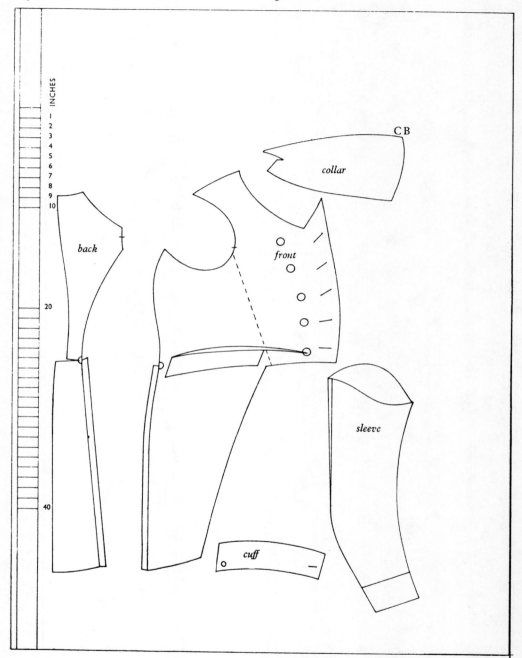

DIAGRAM XXXVIII

DRESS-COAT *c.* 1825. Black woollen cloth. All the edges are cut and the centre front body faced with the same cloth. The chest is padded and the rolled 'horse-collar' very heavily stiffened. The revers have the 'M' notch which appeared *c.* 1803 and is seen until *c.* 1850, and even later on evening coats. *Private Collection*

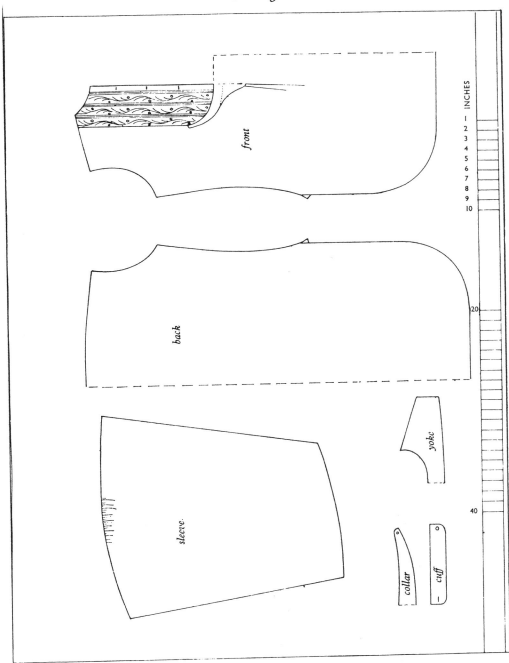

DIAGRAM XXXIX

EVENING DRESS SHIRT *c.* 1870. This shaped cut dates from the second half of the nineteenth century. The pleated or tucked bibbed front appeared *c.* 1820, from 1850 it was starched and after 1870 was usually plain. Yokes from *c.* 1840. *Private Collection*

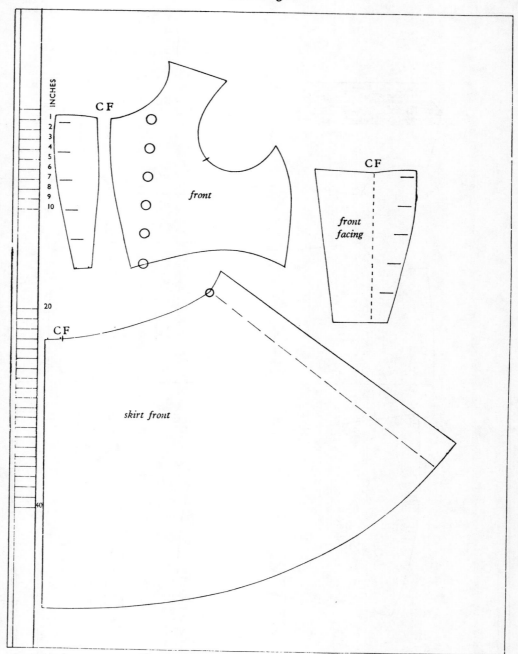

DIAGRAM XL

FROCK-COAT. Light fawn woollen cloth. The body of the coat is unlined but the front skirts are lined with cotton. Collar and rever facings are of a darker fawn velvet. Centre fronts, centre back skirts, cape, bottom of sleeve and pocket flaps are bound in narrow darker fawn silk. Buttons the same colour in basket-weave. *Victoria and Albert Museum*

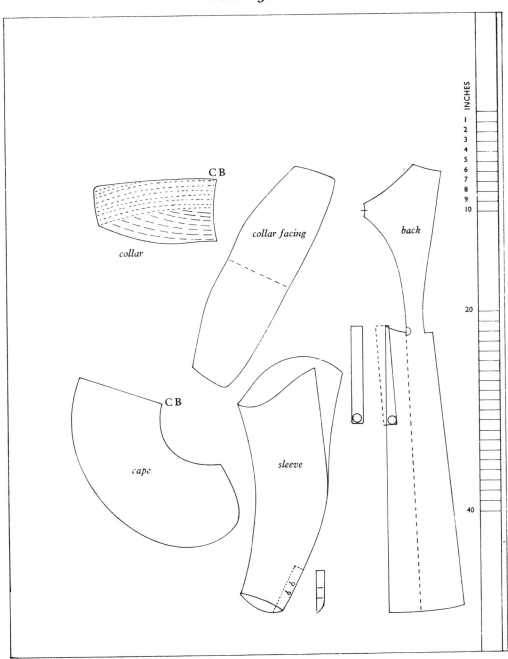

C B

collar

collar facing

back

INCHES
1
2
3
4
5
6
7
8
9
10

20

C B

cape

sleeve

40

DIAGRAM XL

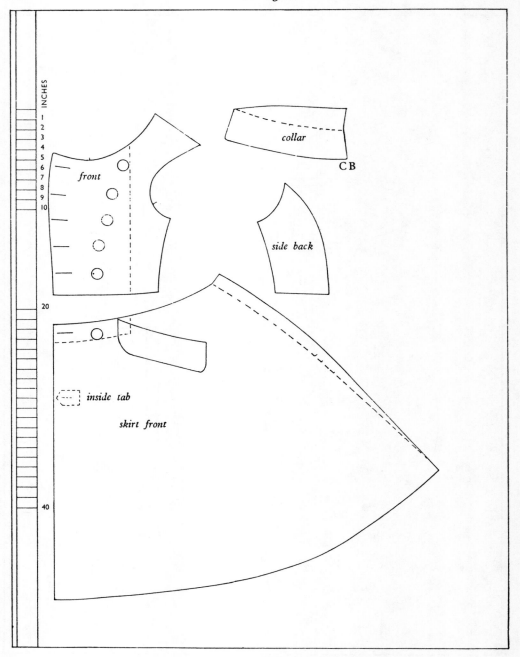

INCHES
1
2
3
4
5
6
7
8
9
10

20

40

collar

C B

front

side back

inside tab

skirt front

DIAGRAM XLI

FROCK-COAT *c.* 1840. Dark brown heavily-milled woollen cloth. All edges cut. Sleeves and front skirts lined heavy cotton. The centre fronts of the body and the collar are faced with the same cloth. This coat has the side back pieces which are retained in all subsequent tail or skirted coats. *Private Collection*

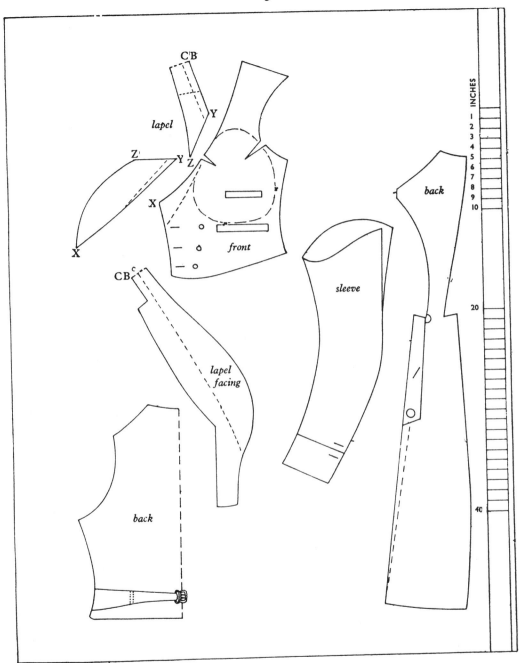

INCHES

DIAGRAM XLII

WAISTCOAT *c.* 1840. Grey moiré silk. The fronts are darted to fit over the padding which gives the fashionable round-chested shape. *Private Collection*

Nineteenth-century Tailoring

When, at the beginning of the nineteenth century, the guiding principle of English style in tailoring became concentrated in cut and fit, the inadequacy of the general practice of cutting by patterns was realized and tailors began their search for a system whereby they could draft out garments which would fit well and yet retain their style and elegance. This search led to a revolution in the art of cutting, and was probably sparked off by the invention of the tape measure early in the nineteenth century.

The origin of the tape measure is unknown, though there were several tailors who claimed to be its inventor. One of them wrote: 'I am well known to the trade, and can say without fear or contradiction that I was the first person who used the inch measure and square, and reduced the trade of a tailor to a system. . . . When I first began to use the inch measure I was laughed at and ridiculed by the trade in general, as being of no utility.' It was probably only by the second quarter of the century that the tape measure was generally accepted. The use of the tape measure, a yard long, and marked out in inches, drew attention to the comparative relations that exist between the various parts of the body. It was found that the length to the waist was half, the chest width one-third, the back one-third, the scye one-third, and the side length of the body one-fourth, of the breast measurement taken under the arms round the body. From these mathematical observations the tailor worked out the first simple drafting system and so began an entirely new approach to cutting, based on the application of geometrical rules and principles to the anatomical proportions of the human figure.

Whereas early literature on tailoring is extremely rare, this new scientific approach brought tailors into print, each one advocating his own particular system. The early ones are very simple and 'so brief, and mysterious that it is almost impossible for any person (if his intellect be ever so good) to gain but little information from them'. But tailors, whether they published their results or not, were slowly progressing along the new lines, and the intelligent ones soon realized that the simple breast measure system was only suitable for well-proportioned figures, and that in most cases additional measurements were necessary.

In the middle of the nineteenth century a much more serious study of the problem was undertaken by a German mathematician, Dr. Henry Wampen. Dr. Wampen was interested in the scientific proportions of Greek statues, and his tailor, who had seen his diagrams, encouraged him to put his knowledge to practical use. In 1834 he published *The Mathematical Art of Cutting Garments According to the Different Formation of Men's Bodies*. His main work, however, was entitled *Mathematical Instructions in Constructing Models for Draping the Human Figure*, 1863. His principles are, briefly, that as everybody in nature possesses the proportion of height and breadth, these must both be taken into consideration when covering the human figure. He divided his work into (1) Anatomy; (2) Anthropometry (man-measurement); (3) Construction of Models—to drape the human figure from the proportionate model to a large series of models to suit various figures, both in regard to style, and normal and abnormal formations. This is a scientific text-book rather than a suitable guide for tailors, but a great part of the knowledge it contained was of practical value and was applied to various systems. He also introduced the principle known as gradation.

The old system of cutting from patterns continued but the pattern blocks were now drafted from some basic system and adapted to the measurements and anatomy of the individual customer. For wholesale mass production these patterns were scaled to suit the main figure types. This method is also suitable for historical costume cutting for the theatre, etc. A tight-fitting body block and also a breeches block pattern, would be very useful in drafting out the diagrams of early suits as given in this book.

Although tremendous progress has been made no system is infallible: the human body is of such infinite variety, structurally and mathematically, that covering it is still a challenge to the tailor's skill. M. Boullay's advice in the seventeenth century: 'Observe well a man before measuring him' still holds good, and is repeated by a modern authority: 'Knowledge of human formation, build and stance is a necessary acquisition of the cutter who wishes to lay a claim to being a sartorial artist.'

Cutting out a garment, though the most important part, is by no means the whole art of tailoring. The putting together of a garment—the subtleties of inter-linings, padding, pressing, sewing, etc.—is not fully appreciated by the layman, whose apparent muscles and sinews are often provided by the tailor's canvas and wadding.

The scientific approach has made tailoring a highly skilled profession, and the various systems which have been published from the early nineteenth century down to the present day make such technical reading that they can only be appreciated by the trained specialist. Those interested in early drafting methods should consult *The History of the Art of Cutting in England*, Edward B. Giles, London, 1887. He gives an excellent account of the development and evolution of the various systems, with numerous quotations as well as illustrations, from early literature on tailoring. Since the second half of the nineteenth century there has been a continuous stream of trade journals and books on the subject.

In conclusion, it may be said that this development of the ancient craft of tailoring

PROFESSIONAL PRIDE.

Smart Tailor (to dissatisfied Customer). "I MUST ASK YOU JUST TO BEAR IN MIND, SIR, THAT TAILORING HAS NOT YET BEEN BROUGHT DOWN TO *THE LEVEL OF ONE OF THE EXACT SCIENCES !*"

has produced well-cut, well-fitted and well-made clothes, and, applied to mass production, has made them available to a vast public. But is it not possible that laying material on a drawing-board, treating cutting as just another engineering problem, by concentrating on the purely technical achievements of fitting an awkward object, has had a stultifying effect on the design of men's clothes? Hasn't something been lost, the old creative spirit stifled, all endearing extravagances ruled out? The skill of the tailor has now reached such an extremely high technical level that he has become a mathematician rather than an inventive artist!

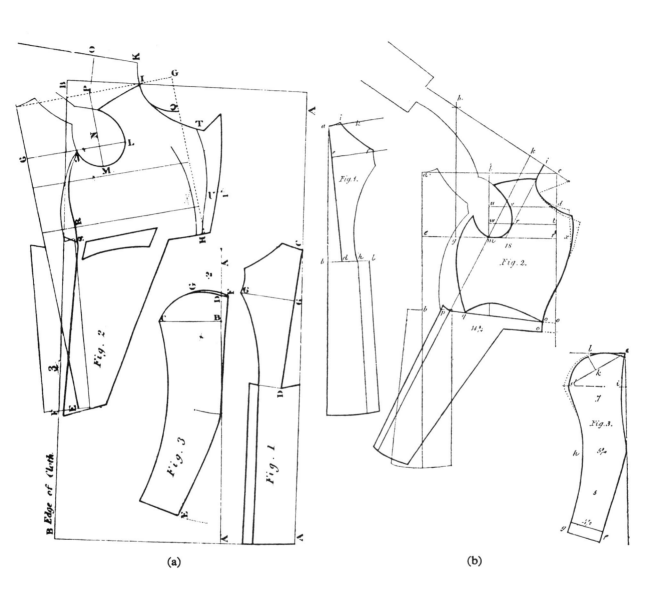

(a) (b)

11. (a) *The Tailors' Friendly Instructor*, J. Wyatt, London, 1822.
Dress-coat.
(b) *The Art of Cutting on Scientific Principles*, London, 1833.
Dress-coat—the front waist seam has been introduced.

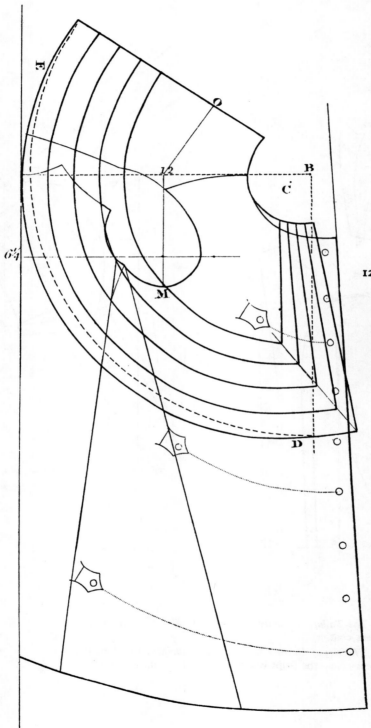

12. *The Tailors' Friendly Instructor.*

Box coat—'Coats of this description are generally cut three or four inches larger than the size of the person, that they may wrap over one or more coats with ease.'

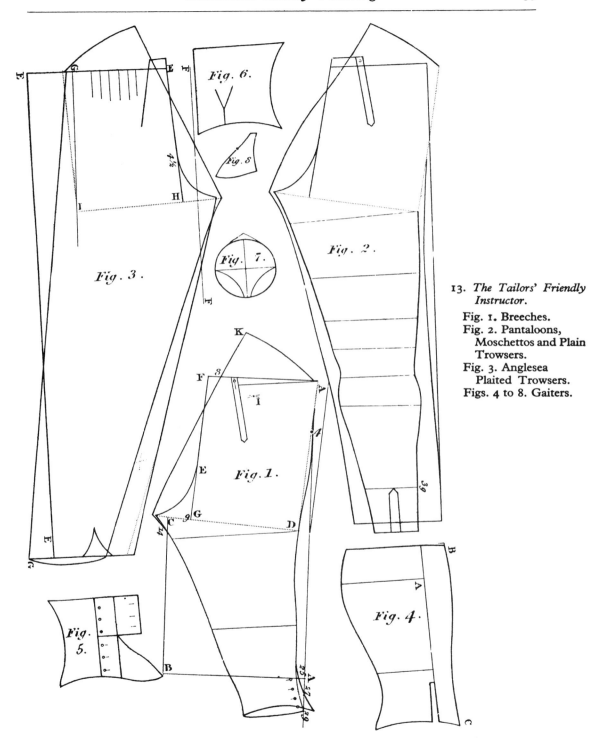

13. *The Tailors' Friendly Instructor*.

Fig. 1. Breeches.
Fig. 2. Pantaloons, Moschettos and Plain Trowsers.
Fig. 3. Anglesea Plaited Trowsers.
Figs. 4 to 8. Gaiters.

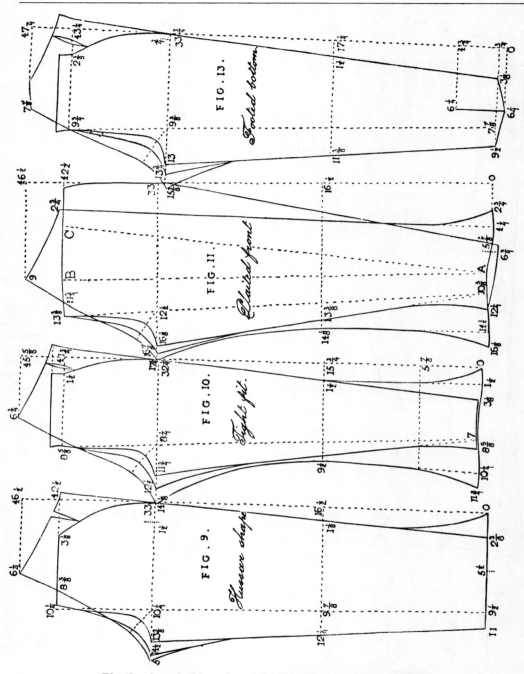

14. *The Gentleman's Magazine of Fashion*, January, 1850. Trousers.

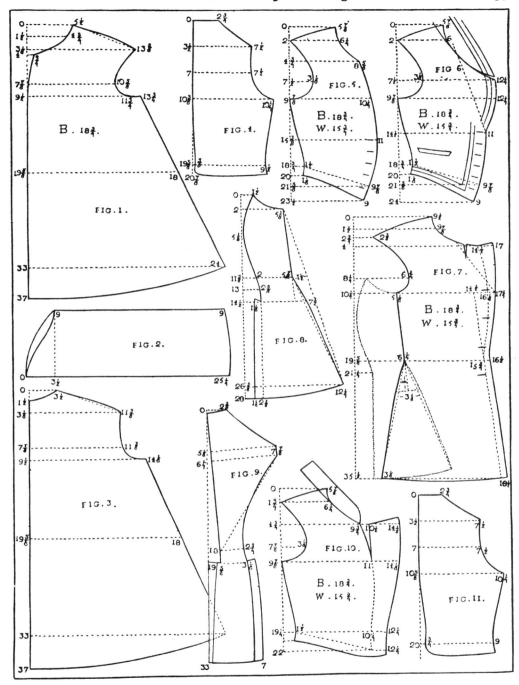

15. *The Gentleman's Magazine of Fashion*, October 1850.
   Figs. 1, 2, 3.   Nepaulese driving coat.
   Figs. 4, 5.   Dress waistcoat—straight form.
   Figs. 4, 6.   Dress waistcoat—shawl form.
   Figs. 7, 8, 9.   Windsor hunting frock—also worn in black or dark colours as
          ordinary frock-coat.
   Figs. 10, 11.   Double-breasted waistcoat.

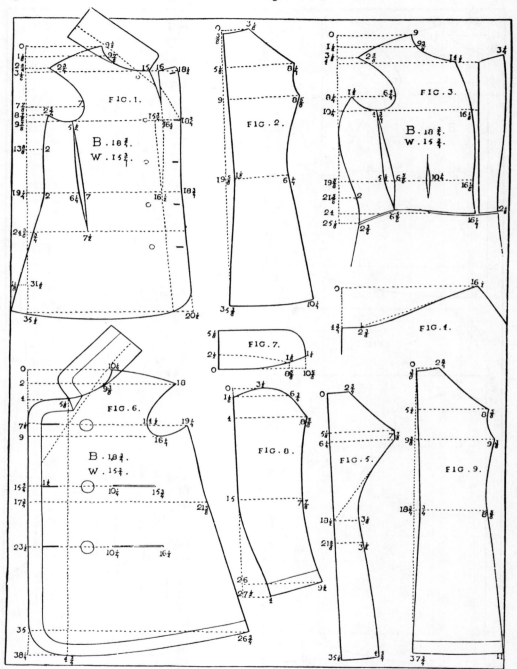

16. *The Gentleman's Magazine of Fashion,* November 1850.
Figs. 1, 2.   Double-breasted top-coat.
Figs. 3, 4, 5.   Double-breasted top-coat.
Figs. 6, 7, 8, 9.   Driving coat.

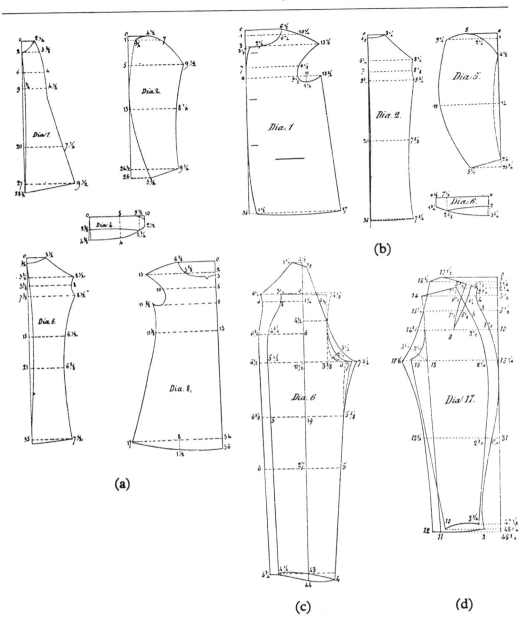

(a)

(b)

(c)

(d)

17. *The Gazette of Fashion.*
April 1859. (a) Dia. 1, 2, 4, 6, 8. New lounge jacket.
February 1861. (b) Dia. 1, 2, 5, 6. Tweedside jacket.
May 1860. (c) Dia. 6. Morning trousers.
August 1861. (d) Dia. 17. 'Peg-top' trousers.

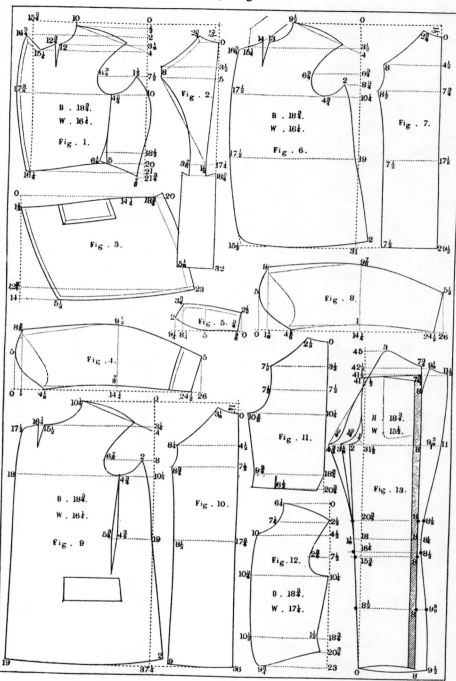

18. *The Gentleman's Magazine of Fashion*, April 1869.
    Figs. 1, 2, 3, 4, 5.   Sutherland morning coat.
    Figs. 6, 7.   Lounging or morning jacket.
    Figs. 8, 9, 10.   Single-breasted summer paletot.
    Figs. 11, 12.   Straight waistcoat without collar.
    Figs. 13.   Trousers with bands at the sides.

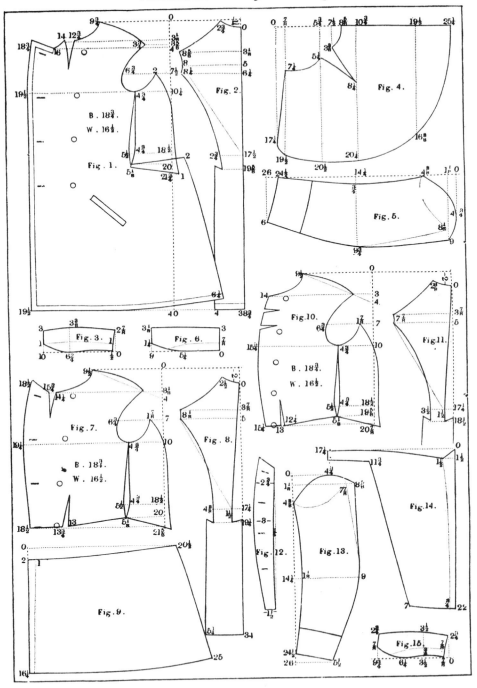

19. *The Gentleman's Magazine of Fashion*, February, 1870.
  Figs. 1, 2, 3, 4, 5.   Gladstone overcoat with cape.
  Figs. 6, 7, 8, 9, 13.   Double-breasted frock-coat for winter.
  Figs. 10, 11, 12, 13, 14, 15. Dress-coat.

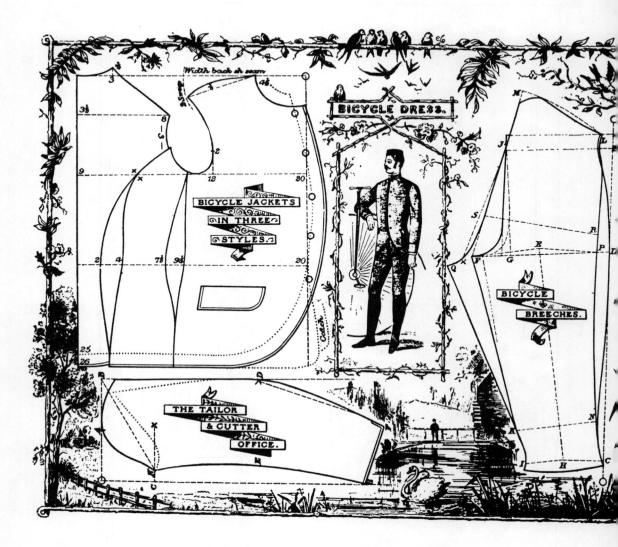

20. *The Tailor and Cutter*, June 1886.

'Bicycle dresses are principally worn by the younger members of society, such as youths and young men who have not arrived at that time of life when the figure begins to grow obese and, therefore, what is wanted in this class of dress is smartness and go.'

1890. 'The Bicycle dress is no longer the patrol jacket and tight knee breeches, instead, a Norfolk or Lounge Jacket and Knickerbockers.'

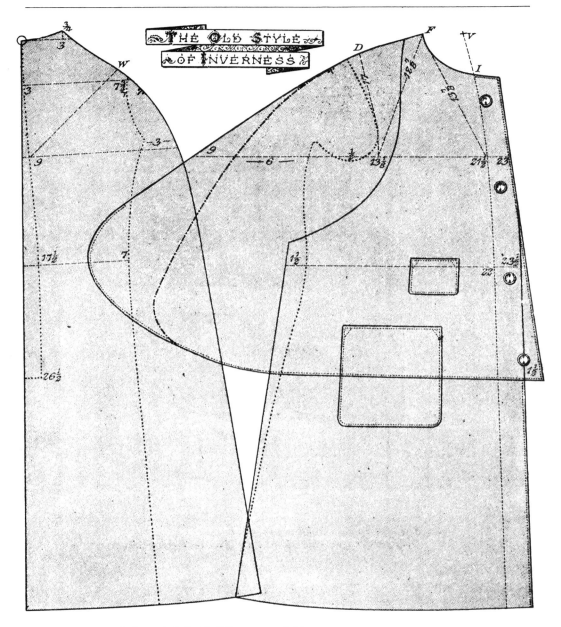

21. *The Cutter's Practical Guide*, Vincent, *c.* 1888.
The Inverness cape appeared in the late '50's and was a very popular type of over-garment until the end of the century.

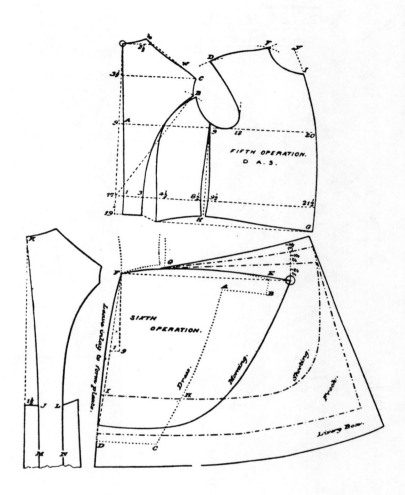

22. *The Cutter's Practical Guide, c.* 1893.
Basic coat shapes—the dotted lines give the various skirt styles.

PLATE 18

1802. French Engraving. Variations in style—top-boots and Hessians, top-hats and chapeau-bras, wigs and cropped hair, etc.

PLATE 19
c. 1820. James Gillray. Caricature
Faces painted deepest brown,
  Waistcoats strip'd and gaudy;
Sleeves, thrice doubled, thick with down,
  And stays, to brace the body.

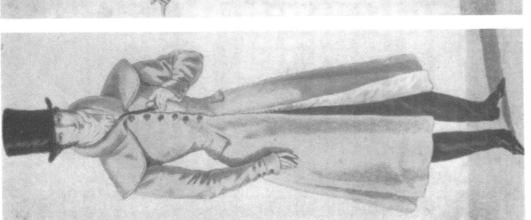

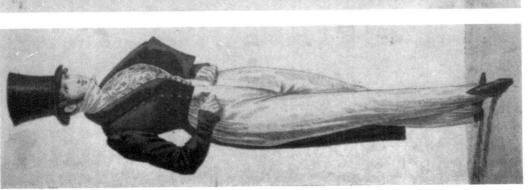

PLATE 20

(*left*) 1820's. Day dress-coat, worn with Cossack trousers. (*centre*) 1820's. Top frock-coat. (*right*) 1820's. Evening dress-coat, worn with pantaloons and stock

PLATE 21

. 1829. A great-coat and a frock-coat—trousers were usually worn with these coats, except in the evening when pantaloons were more formal wear

PLATE 22

1846. A frock-coat and a riding or morning coat—waists much longer but still very tight

PLATE 23

1856. A loose paletot and two frock coats—the line has straightened and the collar and neck-tie narrowed

PLATE 24

1859. A morning coat, a chesterfield, and a Tweedside jacket with matching trousers—
the latter is an early appearance of what was to become the lounge suit

PLATE 25

1872. Evening dress—black waistcoats were worn in the 70's and 80's.
'A relic of bygone days; but despite ridicule and opposition, it still
survives, and as far as can be seen at present is likely to do so for years
to come.' (1893)

PLATE 26
1876. Shooting costumes—knee breeches were still worn for sport

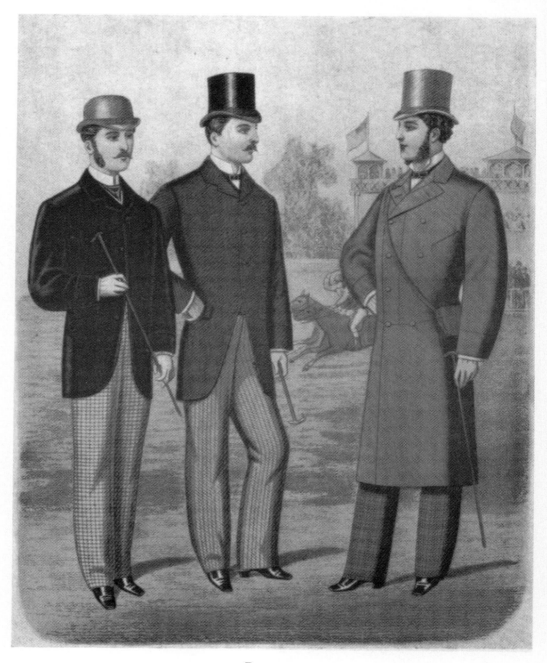

PLATE 27

1880. A lounge jacket, a morning coat, and a top-coat—very straight line, all coats were
buttoned high, collars and ties were at their narrowest

PLATE 28

1891. A frock-coat. 'Usually made to just clear the knee but now
worn much longer. From 40–42 inches for a figure 5 feet 9 inches.'
Nearly always in black but grey worsted became smart day wear
in the 90's

PLATE 29

1895. A morning coat. 'The coat of the period used for all occasions grave or gay.'—Waists shorter, skirts longer and more cut away

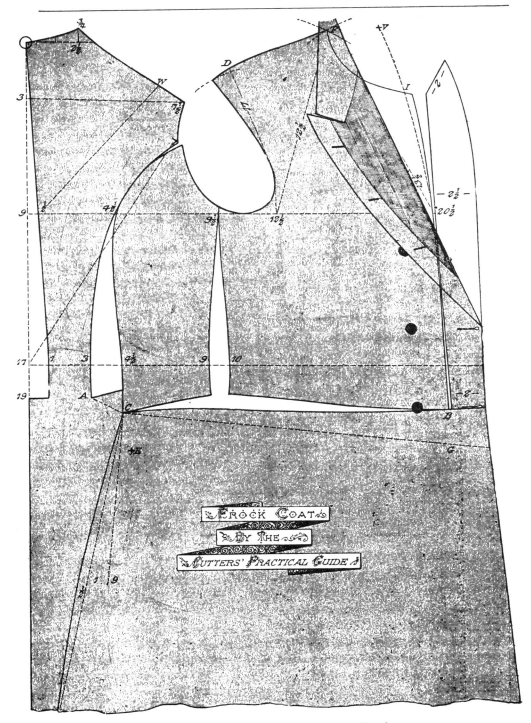

23. *The Cutter's Practical Guide, c.* 1893. Frock-coat.

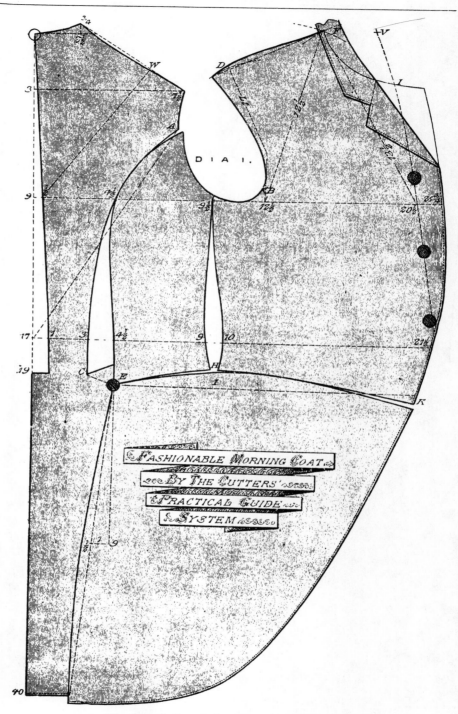

24. *The Cutter's Practical Guide, c.* 1893. Morning coat.

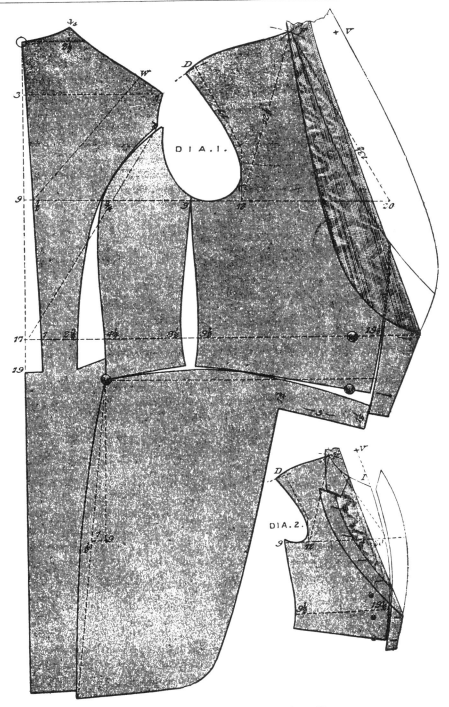

25. *The Cutter's Practical Guide, c.* 1893. Dress-coat.

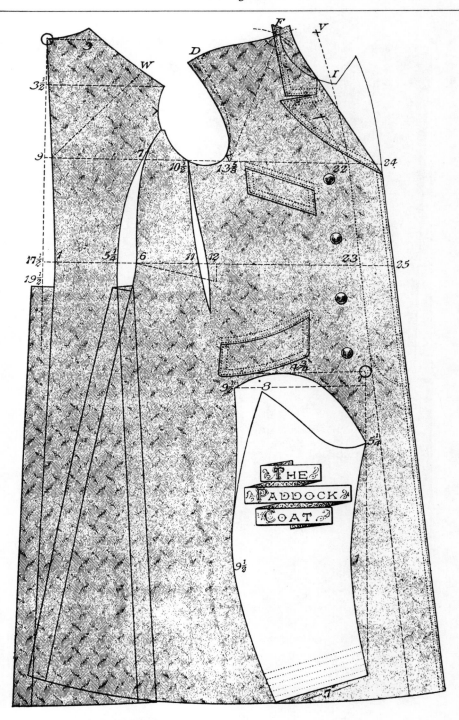

26. *The Cutter's Practical Guide, c.* 1893.
   Paddock coat—a new style designed to cater for the sporting fraternity.

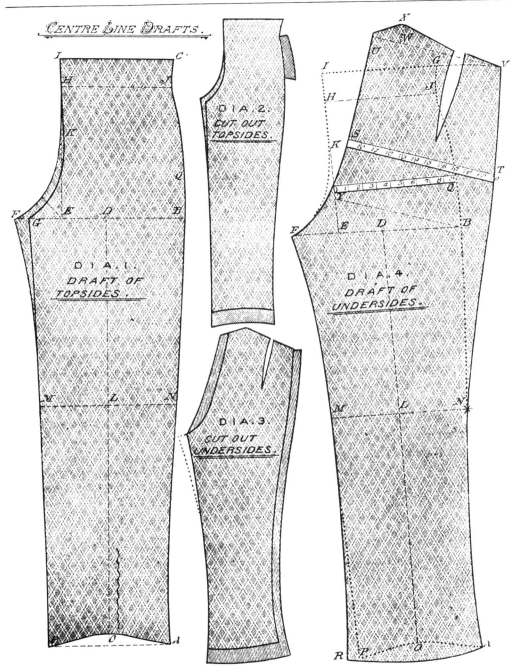

27. *The Cutter's Practical Guide, c.* 1893. Trousers.

Quotations from Contemporary Sources

———————————•××•❂•××•———————————

1800

September—The fashionable colours worn by gentlemen are grey, and all deep colours; such as dark green, bottle green, and dark blue. The neck of the coat is not so long, and the lappels are not so square as before, and are beginning to be cut in a zig-zag kind of shape.

Ladies' Magazine

1802

Paris—The appearance of the men in this theatre was still worse than that of the women—I mean more dirty and slovenly. More of them were powdered than would have been in England, but in great-coats, boots, and had in every way a neglected appearance.

MARY BERRY, *Journals and Correspondence*

EARLY NINETEENTH CENTURY

George Brummell (Retired from Army 1798, left England 1816).

He was a Beau in the literal sense of the word—'fine, handsome'. . . . His chief aim was to avoid anything marked; one of his aphorisms being that the severest mortification a gentleman could incur was to attract observation in the street by his outward appearance. . . .

Brummell was one of the first who revived and improved the taste for dress, and his great innovation was effected upon neckcloths: they were then worn without stiffening of any kind, and bagged out in front, rucking up to the chin in a roll; to remedy this obvious awkwardness and inconvenience, he used to have his slightly starched, and a reasoning mind must allow that there is not much to object to in this reform. He did not, however, like the dandies, test their fitness for use by trying if he could raise three parts of their length by one corner without their bending; yet it appears that if the cravat was not properly tied at the first effort, or inspiring impulse, it was always rejected. His valet was coming downstairs one day with a quantity of tumbled neck-cloths under his arm, and being interrogated on the subject, solemnly replied: 'Oh, they are our failures.' Practice like this, of course, made him perfect, and his tie soon became a model that was imitated, but never equalled.

The method by which this most important result was attained was communicated to me by a friend of his, who had frequently been an eye-witness of the amusing operation.

The collar, which was always fixed to his shirt, was so large that, before being folded down, it completely hid his head and face, and the white neckcloth was at least a foot in height. The first *coup d'archet* was made with the shirt collar, which he folded down to its proper size; and Brummell then standing before the glass, with his chin poked up to the ceiling, by the gentle and gradual declension of his lower jaw, creased the cravat to reasonable dimensions, the form of each succeeding crease being perfected with the shirt which he had just discarded.

His morning dress was similar to that of every other gentleman—Hessians and pantaloons, or topboots and buckskins, with a blue coat and a light or buff-coloured waistcoat; of course fitting to admiration, on the best figure in England; his dress of an evening was a blue coat and white waistcoat, black pantaloons and opera-hat; in fact he was always carefully dressed, but never the slave of fashion.

CAPTAIN JESSE, *The Life of George Brummell*

1808

At this time, the men, as well as their officers, and even the little drummers and pipers had their hair powdered and had queues. . . . There was a hair dresser in each Company. While we were at Malton, the order arrived for the queues and powder to be given up, and a sponge and hair brush to be added to each kit. It was laughable to see the men at afternoon parade, who, having heard of the arrival of the order, saved their hair dressers the trouble of using their scissors, and appeared without queue or powder. Nevertheless they marched off in companies to have their hair properly dressed, and so much better all looked, both officers and men.

SUSAN SIBBALD, *Memoirs*

1816

In 1816, when I was residing in Paris, I used to have all my clothes made by Straub, in the Rue Richelieu. . . . As I went out a great deal into the world, and was every night at some ball or party, I found that knee-breeches were only worn by a few old fogies; trousers and shoes being the usual costume of all the young men of the day. . . .

I mention the following somewhat trivial circumstance to give some notion of the absurd severity in matters of dress and etiquette of Brummell's worthy pupil, the

Prince Regent. A few days after my arrival, I received an invitation to a party at Manchester House, from Lady Hertford, 'to have the honour of meeting the Prince'. I went there dressed 'à la Française', and quite correctly, as I imagined, with white neckcloth and waistcoat, and black trousers, shoes, and silk stockings. The Prince had dined there, and I found him in the octagon-room, surrounded by all the great ladies of the Court. After making my bow, and retiring to the further part of the room, I sat down by the beautiful Lady Heathcote, and had engaged in conversation with her for some time, when Horace Seymour tapped me on the shoulder, and said, 'the "great man"', meaning the Prince, 'is very much surprised that you should have ventured to appear in his presence without knee-breeches. He considers it as a want of proper respect for him'. This very disagreeable hint drove me away from Manchester House in a moment, in no very pleasant mood. . . . In the morning, being on guard, I mentioned what occurred, with some chagrin, to my colonel, Lord Frederick Bentinck, who good-naturedly told me not to take the matter to heart, as it was really of no consequence; and he added—'Depend upon it, Gronow, the Prince, who is a lover of novelty, will wear trousers himself before the year is out, and then you may laugh at him.' Lord Frederick proved a true prophet, for in less than a month I had the satisfaction of seeing 'the finest gentleman in Europe' at a ball at Lady Cholmondeley's, dressed exactly as I had been at Lady Hertford's, and Lord Fife, who was in attendance upon the Prince, congratulated me upon the fact that his royal master had deigned to take example from the young Welshman.

CAPTAIN GRONOW, *Reminiscences*

1818

Reformed Dandy

They explained it by saying, that a dandy was a new term for a buck or a blood; with the difference, that the Dandy aimed rather more at being effeminate, and instead of being a dashing, high-spirited fellow, which 'bloods' generally are, that they only wished to be thought delicate and fine and pretty; that they spent all their money upon hats of a peculiar shape, and great-coats (called by them 'surtouts') of a particular cut, with Wellington boots up to the knees, and trousers just below the calves of the legs, of such as have calves to their legs.

ACKERMANN'S *Repository of Arts*

1821

A dandy is now so bolstered up in collars so lost in trousers, so pinched in the middle, that he can neither have bowels of compassion, expansion of heart, nor fair use of his limbs.

The Hermit in London

1830

Surtout-coats, which are almost all made double-breasted, are nearly the only, or at least the chief undress wear of fashionables westward and eastward. The attention should be most directed in the make of these (which I think, only look well buttoned up close to the throat) to the sit of the skirts, which should be made proportionately full to the closeness of the fit round the waist. This kind of coat should always, to look well, be rather thickly and tastefully padded in front. A velvet collar, too, is becoming; black, blue, and olive are I think, nearly the only colours worn. . . .

Nothing can more improve the look and fit of trousers than double straps; these, with very full Cossack trousers, are more indispensably requisite when the legs are particularly crooked or ill-formed. . . . Regarding tight pantaloons in full dress, though certainly the most popular and becoming in every point of view, yet I would by no means advise any of my readers to assume these without they have at least tolerably good legs. Unless, indeed, they particularly choose to have recourse to art to supply the defects of a crooked or thin leg; in which cases a slight degree of stiffening is absolutely requisite, but the greatest care and circumspection should be used. The finest double-milled black kersey-mere should compose them. . . .

The Hessian is a boot only worn with tight pantaloons, a fashion copied from the military. The top-boot is almost entirely a sporting fashion . . . although they are worn by noblemen and gentlemen occasionally in hunting, they are in general use among the lowest orders, such as jockeys, grooms, butchers, etc. . . . we are apt in London to connect something very low with their appearance. The Wellington, together with the following, are the only boots in general wear; to be anything like the fashion, they should have the toes at least an inch and a half square—such being the custom for both boots and shoes. Bluchers and Collegians are a half-boot. . . . Shoes can only be divided into two classes, long quarters and short quarters, that is dress and undress; the dress being generally termed pumps, and are always adopted in full costume, as being absolutely indispensable to etiquette.

The Whole Art of Dress by a Cavalry Officer

1832

The day before yesterday I was at the first performance of Victor Hugo's tragedy Le Roi s'Amuse. . . . All those present wearing wigs were hissed and booed—among them the duc de Talleyrand.

COUNT APPONYI, *Journal*

1845

To-day Count d'Orsay walked in. I had not seen him for four or five years. Last time he was as gay in his colours as a humming-bird—blue satin cravat, blue velvet waist-coat, cream-coloured coat, lined with velvet of the same hue, trousers also of a bright colour, I forget what; white French gloves, two glorious breast-pins attached by a chain, and length enough of gold watch-guard to have hanged himself in—to-day, in compliment to his five more years, he was all in black and brown—a black satin cravat, a brown velvet waistcoat, a brown coat, some shades darker than the waistcoat, lined with velvet of its own shade, and almost black trousers, one breast-pin—a large pear-shaped pearl set into a little cup of diamonds—and only one fold of gold chain round his neck, tucked together right on the centre of his spacious breast with one magnificent turquoise. Well! that man understood his trade; if it be that of a dandy, nobody can deny that he is a perfect master of it, that he dresses himself with consummate skill! A bungler would have made no allowance for five more years at his time of life; but he had the fine sense to perceive how much better his dress of to-day sets off his slightly enlarged figure and slightly worn complexion, than the humming-bird colours of five years back would have done. Poor d'Orsay! he was born to have been something better than even the king of dandies.

JANE WELSH CARLYLE, *Letters and Memorials*

1854

Balmoral—We have Lord Burghersh (aged 29) here. . . . He sports considerable whiskers and facial furniture, but no moustache, and is in great good looks, so soldier-like and distinguished.

LADY ELEANOR STANLEY, *Twenty Years at Court*

1858

We see our Swells are partly turning their backs upon the all-round collars, that for so many months past have turned their heads—that is to say, granting the possibility of any one who was immersed inside one of those linen fasteners being able to turn his head at all. . . . The present lawn enclosure is by no means so high, allowing a larger slice of the neck to be exposed to the admiring gaze of the fair equestrians of Rotten Row. The outer rim is doubled down over the edge of the shoe-tie that still does gorge-duty instead of a neck-kerchief. Sometimes the shoe-tie is run through a handsome ring, and the ends allowed to dangle elegantly in front.

Punch

1887

Probably in no public assemblage is the dress of the company more uniformly dull and uninteresting than in the House of Commons. Silk hats and Frock coats held undisputed sway so long, that when some of the more daring spirits ventured to present themselves in Morning coats, the sticklers for decorum were alarmed at the innovation and prophesied the downfall of the empire. Since then, things have gone from bad to worse; members are not only seen with Morning coats, but many have adopted the fashion of using two hats—an ancient silk of antique pattern to denote possession of a certain seat, and a low felt or 'pot hat' for wear in and about the lobbies of the house. Several members have long been known to have very decided opinions against what has hitherto been considered to be the correct thing in dress, and have frequently caused a small sensation by appearing in homespun or light Scotch tweeds.

It may interest my readers to know how Mr. Gladstone looked last week, when he made his famous speech against the Coercion Bill. He wore a new black Frock coat, a low buttoning waistcoat, showing a large expanse of shirt front, which is now as well known a ceremonial uniform, as the wig and gown of the Lord Chancellor; and in his button hole was a rose, which is also part of his full dress attire. His large white linen collar, of which the comic papers never omit a caricature, contrasted with his ashen countenance, and gave him the appearance quite the old man.

The Tailor & Cutter

LAST HALF OF THE NINETEENTH CENTURY

As late as the fifties quite a number of peers wore blue coats and brass buttons. Lord Redesdale, for instance, wore a swallow-tailed blue coat with brass buttons, a white necktie and shoes tied with a bow of black ribbon. Nobody ever saw him in any other suit except at a levée. On the whole there has been comparatively little change in gentlemen's dress during the last half-century, though, of course, minor variations have been frequent. Not so very many years ago quite a number of men wore white duck trousers with a frock-coat in summer. The ducks seem now to have totally disappeared whilst I fear the frock-coat is in a fair way to follow them. The hideous, though convenient, cloth cap is a quite modern invention, as was the dinner jacket, which appears after a hard fight to have been conquered by the old swallow-tailed evening coat, which was probably never so firmly established in public favour as it is to-day. The top-hat, though threatened, still holds its own. A great change has taken place in the shape of this headgear since the sixties, when it was far higher than it is now, and thoroughly deserved the appellation of 'stove-pipe', which the Americans, I believe, still call it. During the sixties there was a craze amongst men for large and loud checks and plaids. Some people carried this to a great extreme. The modern tendency would appear to be to suppress all eccentricity of colour or cut in man's dress. In fact, the whole object of a well-dressed gentleman is now to escape notice by the unobtrusive nature of his well-cut clothes. This was not always the case in the past, when West End tailors permitted themselves various extravagancies.

In the fifties the sleeves of men's coats began to be made very full indeed. At last they became almost gigot sleeves, which caused it to be said that the 'peg-tops' (as the full trousers then fashionable were called) were leaving the gentlemen's legs, and taking shelter under their arms.

In my early childhood there were still men living, who had not abandoned the eighteenth-century fashion of wearing a wig. This custom, indeed, did not entirely die out with the coming of the nineteenth century, some old-fashioned people continuing to wear these head-coverings as late as the early thirties. The last man to wear a pigtail is said to have been one of the Cambridge dons, who retained it as late as the year 1835. The higher clergy did not abandon their wigs till a somewhat later date.

LADY DOROTHY NEVILL, *Reminiscences under Five Reigns*

1882

Perhaps one of the most difficult things for us to do is to choose a notable and joyous dress for men. There would be more joy in life, if we were to accustom ourselves to use all the beautiful colours we can in fashioning our own clothes. . . . At present we have lost all nobility of dress and, in doing so, have almost annihilated the modern sculptor. And, in looking around at the figures which adorn our parks, one could almost wish that we had completely killed the whole art. To see the frockcoat of the drawing-room done in bronze, or the double waistcoat perpetuated in marble, adds a new horror to death.

OSCAR WILDE, *Essays and Lectures*

Bibliography

1589 ALCEGA, Juaan de, *Libro de Geometria y Traca*
1618 LA ROCHA BURGUEN, F. de, *Geometria y Traca*
1671 BOULLAY, Le Sieur Benist, *Le Tailleur Sincère*
1688 HOLMES, Randle, Academy of Armoury
1769 GARSAULT, F. A. de, *Description des Arts et Métiers, L'Art du Tailleur*
1771 DIDEROT, *Encyclopédie, Tome IX, Tailleur d'Habits*
1787 PANCKOUCKE, *Encyclopédie*
1796 *The Taylor's Complete Guide*
1817 GOLDING, *Tailor's Assistant*
1822 WYATT, *The Tailor's Friendly Instructor*
1828 LE BLANC, H., *The Art of Tying the Cravat*
1830 *The Whole Art of Dress*
1835 HEARN, W., *The Tailor's Masterpiece*
1838 CANNEVA, M., *Livre du Tailleur*
1845 COUTS, J., *Guide to Cutting*
1863 MINISTER, *Guide to Cutting*
1875 COMPAING and DEVERE, *The Tailor's Guide*
1887 GILES, E. B., *History of the Art of Cutting*
1893 VINCENT, W. D. F., *The Cutter's Practical Guide*
Journals: *Gentleman's Magazine of Fashion*, 1829–50; *Minister's Gazette of Fashion*, 1857–1865;
    West-End Gazette of Fashion, 1865–1877; *Tailor & Cutter*, 1868–1900
BOEHN, Max von, *Modes and Manners*
CHRISTENSEN, Sigrid Flamand, *De Danske Kongers Kronologiske Samling paa Rosenborg*
CUNNINGTON, C. Willett, *Handbook of English Costume in the 17th Century; Handbook of English
    Costume in the 18th Century; Handbook of English Costume in the 19th Century*
DAVENPORT, M., *The Book of Costume*
EKSTRAND, Gudrun, *Karl X Gustavs Dräkter*
FAIRHOLT, F. W., *Costume in England*
KELLY, F. M. and SCHWABE, R., *Historic Costume*
LELOIR, Maurice, *Histoire du Costume*, VIII, IX, X, XI, XII
LAVER, James, *Clothes*
MASNER, Karl, *Kostümausstellung*
QUICHERAT, J., *Costume en France*
RUPPERT, J., *Le Costume*

MUSEUMS WITH COSTUME COLLECTIONS

GREAT BRITAIN

BATH: Assembly Rooms (Mrs. Langley Moore's Collection).
LONDON: Victoria and Albert Museum.
        London Museum.
MANCHESTER: The Gallery of English Costume.
  Many provincial museums have costume collections—Belfast, Birmingham, Bristol, Cardiff,
Edinburgh, Exeter, Glasgow, Hereford, Ipswich, Leeds, Leicester, Norwich, Taunton, Nottingham, York, etc.

CONTINENTAL

DENMARK: Royal Collection of Costume, Rosenborg.
FRANCE: Musée du Costume de la Ville de Paris (Annexe du Musée Carnavalet).
       Centre de Documentation du Costume de la Chambre de Commerce de Paris.
GERMANY: Historical Museum, Dresden.
         National Museum, Munich.
         National Museum, Nuremberg.
HOLLAND: Costume Museum, The Hague.
SWEDEN: Nordic Museum, Stockholm.

Artists, Engravers, Illustrators, etc., for Costume Reference

——————❦❦✦❧❦✦❧❦·o——————

Nicholas Hilliard	1547–1619	J. B. S. Chardin	1699–1779
Isaac Oliver	–1617	Jean Rigaud	1700–1754
François Pourbus	1569–1622	Pietro Longhi	1702–1785
Marc Gheeraerts	1562?–1636	Quentin de la Tour	1704–1788
Paul van Somer	1576?–1621	Francis Hayman	1708–1776
Daniel Mytens	1590?–1647	Arthur Devis	1711–1787
Antoine le Nain ⎫	1588?–1648	Allan Ramsay	1713–1784
Louis ⎬ Brothers	1593?–1648	Sir Joshua Reynolds	1723–1792
Mathieu ⎭	1607?–1677	Paul Sandby	1725–1809
Jacques Callot	1592–1635	Daniel Chodowiecki	1726–1801
Georges de la Tour	1593–1632	Thomas Gainsborough	1727–1788
Crispin van der Passe	1597?–1670?	John Zoffany	1733–1810
Anthony van Dyke	1599–1641	George Romney	1734–1802
Saint-Igny	–1645?	A. de Saint-Aubin	1736–1807
Abraham Bosse	1602–1676	Jean-Michel Moreau	
Samuel Cooper	1609–1672	(le Jeune)	1741–1814
William Dobson	1611–1646	Richard Cosway	1742–1821
Pierre Mignard	1612–1695	Jacques-Louis David	1748–1825
Gerard Terborch	1617–1681	Francesco Goya	1746–1828
John Michael Wright	1617–1700?	John Downman	1750–1824
Sir Peter Lely	1618–1680	Philibert Lois Debucourt	1755–1832
Jean le Pautre	1618–1682	Elisabeth Louise Vigée-	
Charles le Brun	1619–1696	Lebrun	1755–1842
Robert Nanteuil	1623?–1678	Thomas Rowlandson	1756–1827
Nicholas Bonnart ⎫	1637–1718	James Gillray	1757–1815
Henri ⎪	1642–1711	Carle Vernet	1758–1836
Robert ⎬ Brothers	1652–1729	Horace Vernet (son)	1789–1863
Jean-Baptiste ⎭	1654–1726	Louis-Léopold Boilly	1761–1845
Sir Godfrey Kneller	1649–1723	George Morland	1763–1804
Nicholas de Largillière	1656–1746	Jean-Baptiste Isaby	1767–1855
Marcellus Laroon	1653–1702	Sir Thomas Lawrence	1769–1830
Marcellus Laroon (son)	1679–1774	François Gérard	1770–1837
Jean de Saint-Jean	?–?	Jean-Antoine Gros	1771–1835
Antoine Trouvain	1656–1768	Jean-Auguste Ingres	1780–1867
Bernard Picart	1673–1733	Sir David Wilkie	1785–1841
Jean Ranc	1674–1735	Théodore Géricault	1791–1824
Jean François de Troy	1679–1752	George Cruikshank	1792–1878
Antoine Watteau	1684–1721	Constantin Guys	1802–1892
Charles Cochin	1688–1754	Gavarini	1804–1866
Charles Cochin (son)	1715–1790	Franz Xavier Winterhalter	1806–1873
Nicholas Lancret	1690–1745	John Leech	1817–1864
Joseph Highmore	1692–1780	William Powell Frith	1819–1909
William Hogarth	1697–1764	George Du Maurier	1834–1896
Gawen Hamilton	1698–1737	John Singer Sargent	1856–1925
Hubert-François Gravelot	1699–1773	Charles Dana Gibson	1867–1944

With a few exceptions these artists were working in England and France.

Index